Writing Nonfiction That Sells

Other Books by Samm Sinclair Baker
The Complete Scarsdale Medical Diet
The Doctor's Quick Weight Loss Diet
The Doctor's Quick Inches-Off Diet
The Doctor's Quick Teenage Diet
The Doctor's Quick Weight Loss Diet Cookbook
Dr. Stillman's 14-Day Shape-Up Program
Erotic Focus (on Sex)
Family Treasury of Art
Delicious Quick-Trim Diet
Reading Faces
Conscious Happiness: How to Get the Most Out of Living
The Permissible Lie: The Inside Truth About Advertising
Lifetime Fitness
"Doctor, Make Me Beautiful!"
Straight Talk to Parents
Your Key to Creative Thinking
Answers to Your Skin Problems
How to Protect Yourself Today
Vigor for Men
Casebook of Successful Ideas
How to be a Self-Starter
How to be an Optimist
Miracle Gardening Encyclopedia
Miracle Gardening
Samm Baker's Clear & Simple Gardening Handbook
Indoor & Outdoor Grow-It Book
Gardening Do's & Don't's
One Touch of Blood
Murder (Martini), Very Dry
Love Me, She's Dead

WRITING NONFICTION THAT SELLS

Samm Sinclair Baker

Cincinnati, Ohio

Library of Congress Cataloging in Publication Data
Baker, Samm Sinclair.
  Writing nonfiction that sells.
  Includes index.
  1. Authorship. I. Title.
PN145.B36   1986   808'.02   86-1318
ISBN 0-89879-212-6

*Dedicated to
Michael and Caleb
and all who will
write the future
for themselves
and the world.*

Contents

Chapter One

WHY THIS BOOK WILL HELP YOU MAKE MONEY WRITING

Every word in this book works toward one purpose: *to help you make money from your writing*. No vague theorizing, confusing double-talk, or evasions. My recommendations here are openly and honestly "commercial"—to help you turn rejection into acceptance, to earn more and more from your writing.

While this book focuses primarily on how to make money writing nonfiction, most of the hundreds of ways work in writing and selling *fiction* as well. I've proved that with my published novels, novelettes, and short stories . . . along with nonfiction books, articles, television, film, and other categories of writing. I even organize and use similar work methods (Chapter VI) to produce salable fiction as well as nonfiction. You can do the same.

In my varied classes and lectures, I've challenged participants: *"If you can write your name, you can make money writing."* They and I have proved repeatedly that my clear, simple, how-to directions work. The instructions are all here, ready for you to use starting at once and for permanent reference.

LEARN WHAT MISTAKES TO AVOID

You'll learn here exactly what mistakes to avoid—and how to write it right—so you can overcome errors you didn't recognize heretofore. You can bank on this because I remember my own problems as a beginner as vividly as if they were happening today. There was so much I wanted and needed to know to score sales instead of hundreds of turndowns. After innumerable articles and thirty books, I've analyzed what I did wrong and give you my findings.

This new know-how will guide you to make relatively simple, swift changes leading to *sales*. The same simple but decisive facts of writing life keep working for me. Their specific effectiveness is *proved* by many published, selling writers whom I've taught and guided through the years.

I reveal all the effective guidelines to you because we writers are "family," so we share. Every individual I've been able to follow up who used my pointers and wrote enough has become a successful published writer.

INCREASE YOUR WRITING EARNINGS

If your writing is selling some now, the practical information here will help you make *more* money from your efforts. That's true for better-paying articles, books, all kinds of nonfiction subjects, viewpoints, themes. Please regard every recommendation as *increasing your earning power*. (Most of the recommendations work for fiction, too, but nonfiction sales are our primary target.)

To help you most, I draw many practicable examples from my writing experience, not to blow my horn, but to provide *how-to specifics* that I've learned in over forty years of writing nonfiction that sells. Compact, easy-to-digest capsules give you answers to questions directed at me by beginning, intermediate, and professional writers—resulting from queries in face-to-face discussions and courses I have taught at universities, workshops, writers' conferences, and lecture series.

DO RESULTFULLY, DON'T DREAM EMPTILY

From now on, you must set your course, guided by precepts here, added to your talents and aims. Realize fully that your writing will be *doing* and selling, that you'll no longer be fumbling or just dreaming about or yearning to be a successful published writer. My personal expressed writing aim has always been "to help people live happier, more fulfilling lives." In this book, my goal is to help each writer—*you*—to live your happiest, most productive, most rewarding life—*selling what you write.*

I recommend that you refer to this book innumerable times for the rest of your profitable writing life. I certainly will, too, now that the basics are solidly at hand in print to help myself and you to *do*, not just *wish. We all need reminders frequently.*

READ ALL
THE WAYS-THAT-WORK

To use this book most resultfully . . . to become a steadily selling writer with increasing income . . . I urge you to read *all the ways-that-work*, on every page from cover to cover. If you don't, you won't gain maximum benefit.

As you proceed, use a pencil to check those pointers that apply most specifically to your personal wants and needs. Reread them in the future repeatedly to build deep-seated expertise. Each capsule will help you *write to sell* by adding to your knowledge of not only what to do but also what not to do—to score sales and avoid rejections.

Of course you must apply the time and effort in order to reap the rewards. Best-seller author E. L. Doctorow lays it on the line: "Planning to write is not writing. Outlining a book is not writing. Researching is not writing. Talking to people about what you're doing, none of that is writing. Writing is writing."

Certainly planning, outlining, researching, talking—all are part of it, but they're not actual writing. Finally, only writing is writing; you become a writer by writing.

Let's get to work.

Chapter Two

TO SELL, INTEREST THE READER

One of the first questions that writers, beginners and professionals, ask me is this: "How do you manage to write successfully about so many different subjects—dieting, health, gardening, art, sex, education, living happily, analyzing individuals, money-making, business methods, self-protection, and on and on? *Is there a common factor that can help me choose subjects that will sell?*"

I'm glad you asked. Yes, there is one common factor that guides all my nonfiction subjects from Art to Zinnias: I always select *a subject of high self-interest to many readers.* That point unites all my writing. I recommend that before you write on any subject, you ask yourself:

"Is this of high self-interest to enough readers?"

The honest answer to yourself can cut off many rejections which have nothing to do with the *quality* of your writing. It will help keep you from getting turned down because the *subject matter* of your piece is not of sufficient interest to the publication's readers. The following all-important checkpoints will guide you to produce writing that sells.

APPLY THE THREE BASIC CHECKPOINTS

The reasons for your offerings being turned down are usually surprisingly clear and simple *once you know how to identify and cor-*

rect them for your own benefit. You'll gain practical, invaluable
eye-openers by applying the three basic checkpoints which follow; these will be expanded from various illuminating angles
throughout the book.

Utilize these and further checkpoints-to-come in analyzing
all of your nonfiction writing in the future *before* submitting any
for publication. You'll invariably uncover crucial, costly flaws,
and then you'll see exactly how to make necessary changes. Such
revisions often make the difference between sale or turndown.

Checkpoint No. 1: WILL THIS SUBJECT INTEREST ENOUGH READERS?

At a lunch, the great editor of *Good Housekeeping*, John Mack
Carter, enlightened me about editorial needs. He said that there
are three subjects of outstanding interest to most women and
many men today. Readers, he emphasized, are constantly seeking new, usable information about: *Diet . . . Sex . . . Money.*

If you write about these prime subjects—offering fresh,
readily grasped approaches—you'll certainly have a better
chance to sell than if your piece is about "The Prevalence of Fire
Ants in Abyssinia." That's a wild exaggeration on my part in order to make an essential point: *Write what interests most others,
not just what pleases you.*

Of course, you don't have to confine yourself to these three
down-to-earth categories; possibilities are endless, as covered in
detail later. Yet, even within that seeming limitation, the prospects for writing that sells are practically unlimited. For example, consider the many variations, such as:

> *Diet:* "Drop Pounds Now with 12 Delicious New Recipes"
> *Sex:* "Enchanting New Hairstyles Boost Sex Appeal"
> *Money:* "Add Income with Easy New Work-at-Home Ideas"

By studying what has been written on subjects of great and
enduring personal interest to most people, and then applying
your personal creativity, you can provide endless valuable, enlightening "new" helps for readers. On diet, for one, I've written
dozens of articles and seven books to date, which have sold tens of
millions of copies. Each is better than the preceding, of course,

because, like me and any alert individual in every pursuit, you will learn, revise, add, improve. You will get better and better as you write more and more about a subject.

Similarly, on sex, money, or any other topic, do you think there's nothing new under the sun? Has everything been written or said? Of course not! If people didn't learn and improve by doing, we'd all still be living in caves.

You, the writer, must and will find and explain, clarify, and present *the better way* interestingly and informatively. Thus you will sell what you write—no question about it in my experience.

Write what interests them, not just you. In choosing a subject, always bear in mind the old saw: "Feed your pets what *they* want to eat, not what *you* prefer." Similarly, choose a subject that is of high interest to other people, *realizing that editors are people, too.*

Analyze carefully beforehand the desires of the particular audience you're trying to reach. Otherwise, you'll waste time and effort and invite discouragement. Smart subject selection is fundamental if you *write to sell.* Clearly, selling interests you, or you wouldn't be reading this. Likewise, what attracts and involves the reader primarily is his or her self-interest.

Never lose sight of this fundamental point: Write about what people want to read and therefore editors want to buy—not just what *you* want to write and sell. That's a prime keystone of acceptance or rejection.

Gauge reader interest in advance. First, in choosing a subject, assess your selling goal in respect to where it will have the best chance to be published. You have many choices. Consider them carefully with each submission. You can aim at publications with small circulation numbers, moderate, or mass.

It's fine to *think small* and go for smaller-circulation, specialized magazines. Those may make the best sense as being the best markets for beginners. For one reason, there's less competition from known professionals.

You can *think moderate,* targeting your writing at the medium market with sizable but not multimillions in circulation—publications focused on child care, education, gardening, any number of categories.

You can also *think big*, going for mass-market media. Included here, as you undoubtedly know, are the women's mass service magazines: *Family Circle, Woman's Day, Good Housekeeping*, and loads of others that you're aware of or can track down in stores, on newsstands, in directories.

You'll find market listings in various directories such as *Writer's Market*, which provide a good many categories of publications, with names and addresses of those in each group. The *Literary Market Place* lists "Magazines—Classified by Subject Matter." These and other directories are generally available at libraries, or buy your own copy for repeated reference. Listings are usually brought up to date each year.

The one best way to discover what subjects are of greatest interest to readers of a magazine—and therefore to its editors—is to *examine several issues* of the publication. The contents listings tell you what subjects they cover, what writing they are most likely to buy. It almost goes without saying that you'd be wasting time, effort, and money if you sent a piece about machine tools to *Ladies' Home Journal*, for instance (I mention this only because such foolishness occurs—ask any editor).

I hear some writers saying, as I've heard countless times, "I'm better off not competing, but offering a subject that's *different*." Experience proves that in most instances you'd be cutting the sales odds to almost zero. Compete best by writing something creative, fresh, more informative on subjects a magazine covers repeatedly in issues month after month, because they're the topics that interest their readers most. Exceptions? Of course.

"I-I-I" triggers "no-no-no" from editors. A common mistake of beginners is the I-I-I approach: Writing about your personal experiences is usually a mistake unless you're sure the happenings are so remarkable, dramatic, and instructive that they'll appeal to a wide audience. In my activities on the editorial side, I found that the I-I-I approach is common—and generally results in instant rejection when run-of-the-mill experiences are described.

It's safest to get it out of your head that *anything* that happens to you is of interest to others!

I've been there and I assure you: Editors groan when a manuscript begins, "I remember Aunt Clara very well. I loved her deeply, and I'll always treasure sweet memories of her. . . ." Very few magazine readers care about your Aunt Clara or your Uncle Ted unless they're the first to land on the planet Venus or are involved in something else extraordinary.

In contrast, many of the same readers would be interested in a published article that began:

> *The weekend spa business is booming, but what can a brief stay at a spa do for you realistically? Can it help you lose weight, keep on taking off pounds and inches, and stay slim from then on? For the answers, I interviewed five men and five women who had been to various weekend spas a month earlier. Here's what they reported . . . .*

Obviously, your chances of a sale would be infinitely better with the spa piece, which immediately promises valuable information and self-improvement for the reader.

Checkpoint No. 1 is clear: Before you write on any theme, consider the subject through the eyes of the editor, whose responsibility it is to interest, inform, and assist readers most positively. Realize that, as the editor, you must attract enough readers and that you'll buy only pieces which will accomplish that. To sell your writing, *you must fulfill the editor's needs*. That means you must focus on the you-you-you of the reader, not on your personal I-I-I.

Before you protest that you never make that error, check back on your past offerings. You may be surprised at what you find. Certainly, you'll never make that mistake in the future. (Of course, if you're a President's wife or daughter or personal valet, editors and readers will probably gobble up your I-I-I revelations in writing.)

Author's Note

I must emphasize again that the examples and case histories provided from my personal experience are not *I-I-I* but *You-You-You*. My purpose always is to help inform and instruct you—to demonstrate exactly how you can make money writing most effectively and profitably.

Checkpoint No. 2: ARE YOUR OPENING LINES "READER GRABBERS"?

Another brilliant editor I know, who directs an extremely successful mass-circulation magazine, brought home for the weekend a huge briefcase loaded with nonfiction articles submitted for publication. He said, "Before I take you sailing, help me weed out which of these pieces have possibilities for an issue coming up soon."

I protested, "It will take me forever to get through these."

"You'll be finished in less than an hour," he assured me. "You can usually tell by reading just the first paragraph whether to discard or go further. If the opening sentences don't grab and hook you, reject the whole piece—the writing rarely gets any better." I'd found this to be true also in practically every class I'd taught.

That point is worth reading again, and making it an essential primary double-check rule for everything you write: *If the opening sentences don't grab the reader's (editor's) interest at once, start over until you have a true instant reader grabber.*

Examples of reader grabbers. Here are a couple of instances to scrutinize in order to clarify how much the opening sentences matter in the pieces you write. Again, read them as though you're the editor examining the two following submissions on the same general subject. Based on the opening paragraphs alone, which manuscript would you, the editor, have read with greater attention—and probably have purchased?

> (A) *Everyone in the neighborhood spoke well of Maryann Browne. She could usually be seen sitting in the old rocker on her front porch, swaying slightly as she knitted patiently hour after hour. We were all deeply shocked when we heard that her family doctor, whom we all know, let it be known through the grapevine that she had cancer . . . .*

> (B) *I'm a cancer patient, in the midst of that uneasy purgatory known as remission. After a year that would make the cast of* Dynasty *shake its collective head in disbelief, I am*

trying to get well. I will *get well. That is, if people will let me. The cancer may not kill me. But I'm not at all sure about the public . . . .*

The article that was bought, and appeared in a leading magazine, was "B," of course. As a casual reader idly turning the pages, I found that the opening brief paragraph grabbed me. The writer telling flat out that she is afflicted with the dread disease led me on with the promise of hope in "remission." I was hooked further by the unexpected challenge in the surprising dramatic twist that "the public" might keep her from getting well. The public? That's *me!* Now *I* was involved. How could I possibly stop reading?

It's obvious why I, or you, as editor, if offered a choice, would reject "A," probably without reading any further. Why should I be particularly interested in someone I don't know—Maryann Browne—just because people "spoke well" of her? There's nothing very new or promising about a woman sitting in an old rocker on her front porch, knitting patiently hour after hour. Sure, I (and you) feel deep compassion for anyone with cancer, but that's not enough to *compel* me to read more. Result: rejection. I'll bet that the discouraged writer never realized why her piece didn't sell—as you understand now.

Be creative to cook up reader grabbers. Note carefully this vital self-teaching example to help you avoid rejection slips in the future, or turn your past rejects into sales: A fine professional writer wanted to sell an article on beauty care to one of the best-paying, top-circulation women's magazines. But she knew there was tremendous competition in the beauty article field, not just from other free-lance writers, men and women, but from the publication's staff writers.

She put her creativity to work and sought out one of the most popular photography models, who agreed to coauthorship. Just one problem, as she knew too well: Most women might feel that they couldn't learn from a model who started with "perfect features." So the writer tackled the dilemma head-on with this opening paragraph:

You don't have to be born with perfect features to have a mod-

el's face. [Really? Tell me more . . . .] Many of the world's highly paid models are not necessarily natural beauties, but they have the ability to put their best face forward. That means skin care and carefully applied makeup. I'd like to share with you some of the very special beauty secrets I've learned during my career as a model . . . .

That's the hook—the grabber—the promise from a top model to share her beauty secrets with *you*. Possibly you're asking yourself, "Why didn't I think of a creative idea like that, and write an opening that would make the sale to an editor?" From now on, I hope you will.

Rewrite openings as often as necessary. Don't ever send along any of your writing to a publisher until you're as sure as you can be that you've created a definite reader-grabber start. Make that a must even if it means rewriting dozens of times.

I've reworked the opening paragraphs of my articles as well as my best-selling books up to twenty and more times. I kept revising until I felt as sure as I could be that I'd fashioned an irresistible promise, the hook that would seize and hold the reader.

One of the best examples I know is the start of the best-selling diet book of all time, *The Complete Scarsdale Medical Diet*, which I coauthored with Dr. Herman Tarnower. (This opening has appeared before as a prime specimen of hooking a reader's attention; it's worth repeating as a proven sales maker.) The doctor is speaking:

I, personally, explain the Scarsdale Medical Diet's *phenomenal popularity in two words: "It works." A slim, trim lady said to me recently, "Your diet is beautifully simple, and the results are simply beautiful." I just say, "It works."*

How many readers concerned about overweight can refrain from continuing at this point? A reader grabber like that can work for you. Check your opening lines repeatedly to make sure they convey convincing promise of worthwhile, productive reading ahead.

For fiction too, it's just as important to keep reader grabbers in mind. Here's an example of how to seize editor and reader attention immediately—from the start of a superbly written, highly praised novel, *The Handyman,* by Penelope Mortimer:

> *Gerald Muspratt gave no indication of what he was about to do. He walked over to the french windows in the drawing room to inspect the weather and, without even turning round, died.*

You're "hooked," aren't you? As editor or reader, you can't resist reading on to find out the cause of the man's death, and on and on. From such small beginnings, big sales grow. On the other hand, if your opening lines are a yawn, rejection is likely to follow. Now you know one reason for failure, and you'll avoid this flaw in the future.

Checkpoint No. 3:
HAVE YOU DONE
ENOUGH SELF-EDITING?

"A fine cook knows when to take a dish out of the oven so it's neither underdone nor overcooked," an editor commented. "But most of the scripts I reject are either underwritten—not enough thought and work put into them—or are overwritten, too many words to say too little, not enough careful cutting."

When I've been involved on the editing end, I've found that many twenty-page manuscripts would have been more acceptable if cut to fifteen or even ten pages. Yet, when I've suggested this to earnest individuals, the reaction has usually been, "You want me to cut out what I've worked so hard to put in? The writing is good, isn't it?"

Yes, the writing may be good, but as the cliché affirms, it can be "too much of a good thing." Any word that isn't effective and essential should be eliminated. Stop and think what "edit" means. According to dictionaries, "to edit" means "to make written materials suitable for publication." Ask yourself next time you're about to send out a piece you've written:

"Have I worked this over specifically, so it's 'suitable for publication,' stating exactly what the reader needs and wants to know?"

"Have I been thoroughly diligent, and not too lazy to go back and cut again and again?"

"Am I certain that I've not been too much in love with my own words to edit sufficiently?"

If your answer to all or any one of these questions is not an indisputable "yes" in each case, you know what you must do without hesitation: Revise and rewrite until you're sure the answer to all three is in the affirmative.

Cut-cut-cut mercilessly. A big part of successful professionalism grows from enough self-editing. The material you're reading was far more than three times as long before I cut-cut-cut. I did the cutting to make what you need to know most understandable and useful for you, not yielding to my own lassitude or vanity for an instant. Yes, it hurts to cross out words, paragraphs, pages you've sweated over. But it's essential to successful selling.

After millions of words I've written and sold, I still check every piece according to all three of the preceding basic checkpoints. That discipline keeps working for me. There are other factors that can make or break a sale. Some, such as timing and overstock, are often out of your control. Regardless of such unforeseeable obstacles, these checkpoints, along with the hundreds of other pointers here, can and will work remarkably well for you.

PICTURE THE READER AS YOU WRITE—LITERALLY

Here's another "Exclusive Sales-Making Tip—First Time Ever!" I don't know of any other writer who uses this simple little twist, nor have I ever written about it—because it's pretty far out. Confession time:

When I write an article or book, I usually clip from a magazine a few photos of individuals whom I consider to be "typical" readers on the subject. If I'm writing on diet, the people in the pictures range from a little plump to quite heavy. If my theme is schooling, I'll select a family group picturing Mom, Dad, and a couple of school-age kids. When I write about sex . . . figure that out for yourself.

I like to "see" the people I'm trying to reach and help as actual visible images (propped prominently in sight on my desk). In this way, I find myself better able to "talk" to them and even "listen" to them via my writing.

I call it communication. Others will probably call it weird. In any case, it helps me write what sells. If you're the same kind of nut, perhaps it will help you. Why not try it? One thing sure, it connects you to your prospective readers tangibly.

MILLION DOLLAR TIP: FOCUS ON THE SUBJECT AND MAKE THE SALE

When I was an advertising writer, a client kept teasing for months by promising me a "million-dollar tip guaranteed to make you rich and successful." Finally, he gave me the tip: "To make the sale to a prospective advertising client, *hold his product in your hand* as you make your pitch. If it's a soap account, grip a bar of his soap. Or if he's an automaker, hold a part from one of his cars. That's it—that tip can be worth millions to you."

I felt let down until I realized the true value of what he had conveyed: ***Holding the prospect's product in my hand would keep me centered on what interested him most—his product!*** That act itself would inhibit me from straying from the all-important subject when making any pitch. It worked.

Adapting the "million-dollar tip" to writing, I use this little trick: I write the topic of an article or book on a little tent card which I keep in clear sight on my desk as I proceed.

Samples: "Rock Gardens," to keep me solidly on that subject instead of letting me stray into the vegetable patch. "Fitness for *Women*" when writing a book on healthful procedures for females, not males. "Better Sex" while working on a book on that titillating topic.

There's a card facing me on my desk right now boldly lettered: "Make Money Writing: Writing Nonfiction that SELLS." It helps keep me on target, to ensure that I aim every word at helping you, the reader, most.

BILLION DOLLAR TIP: AS YOU WRITE, BECOME A SPLIT PERSONALITY

Become a split personality! That is, become the *reader* as well as the writer. Make every word you write convey ***what the reader wants and needs to know***. If you learn nothing more than that from this book, it will have been more than worth your while.

By splitting yourself and becoming the reader as you write, you provide the vital information essential to sell the editor, whose own personality is split into being both editor and reader. You keep your attention focused fixedly on the reader's needs and wants—that's the bottom line for checking a hit or a miss.

That one tip is a major key to my success in selling what I write. I learned it as an advertising copywriter years back. When I'd start to write an ad for print, radio, TV, all media, I'd close my eyes and picture myself not as the writer, ***but as the customer in the store or showroom or other purchasing spot, about to buy***. Then I'd tell the customer (me) what she/he wanted and needed to know.

That's exactly what I recommend when writing nonfiction to sell: ***Become the reader*** learning interestingly, clearly, usably, exactly what she/he wants and needs to know.

Now that split-personality method is yours. All you have to do to succeed is to use it, whatever subject you write about.

YOU BECOME YOUR OWN EDITOR

After absorbing the basic checkpoints and all the recommendations in these pages, apply them to the piece of writing you just finished, along with others done in the past that didn't sell. Concentrate on reading line by line objectively with your newly acquired knowledge—*as though you were the editor.*

Now, as editor rather than writer, *you* must decide whether or not to buy the piece for publication. Be ruthlessly honest as you ask yourself: "Is the manuscript faulty according to any or all of the basic checkpoints and others?"

If you find faults—as you will inevitably—revise, rewrite, or start all over again from scratch. It often pays to discard the entire piece if it doesn't measure up. Finally, after you've proceeded, persevered, word by word, through this process, you'll be thrilled by the improvements you make readily, once you realize exactly what is wrong.

That's *self-help in action.* You'll possess and will use this simple method profitably in planning and completing everything you write to sell from now on.

Urgent: Keep Re-examining

To make sales instead of collecting rejections, scrutinize every word before offering an article to make sure that what you've written fulfills these three basic checkpoints:

1. The SUBJECT will interest enough readers.
2. The opening lines are "READER GRABBERS."
3. You have SELF-EDITED objectively and repeatedly.

If you adhere to these three essentials throughout your writing life, you'll make money writing, year after year.

Chapter Three

GETTING IDEAS FOR WRITING THAT SELLS

This has happened to you often, or will: Someone you meet learns that you're a writer and says eagerly, "I have a great idea for an article" (or a book). You may be intrigued, but it's important not to let personal enthusiasm overcome good judgment. This careful, patient approach works for me:

When I'm confronted by what might seem to be a good idea or a great subject, I suspend any decision until I have the time to think about it thoroughly. Then I *write out* a brief summary of my thoughts and the possibilities and sales potential in the idea.

Before any further step, I put the note away, get busy with other writing for a week or two. At the end of that period, I reexamine the jotting analytically—again as the editor and reader, not the writer. Often I realize reluctantly that the idea wouldn't appeal to enough people to result in a sale, my ultimate test.

If you think that's too restrictive, realize that ideas that sell are *not* dull and uncreative, even though they may not strike you first as "different." The one ingredient they must embody is not "cleverness" as such, but abundant interest and information for editors and readers. Toward that end, you can free your imagination and enjoy the writing thoroughly.

Of course, if the "great idea" passes the analysis test outlined, it could be money in the bank. Dig in, then write an article query or make a book presentation. At least you won't be gambling on spur-of-the-moment, half-baked enthusiasm.

ASSESSING "GREAT IDEAS" FOR WRITING BOOKS

Writers, including beginners, are approached in many instances by physicians and other experts to write books with them. (See details later in Chapter 13, "Coauthorship: A Challenging Way to Extra Sales.") Mostly, such individuals, smart as they may be in their own fields, know little about writing and publishing (but too often think they know a lot).

Here's the pattern I follow: If I think there's any substance at all to the idea, I say that I'll think it over. My first question to myself in any case is: *"Will it sell enough?"* I urge you to consider that sales viewpoint *before* you catch fire.

For example, I've been approached by doctors repeatedly to write a book on *diabetes*. After researching the subject enough to get a solid marketing evaluation about it, I've always turned it down. The doctor protests, "But umpty million people are afflicted with diabetes. Millions of diabetics and their families will buy the book. It's a great idea, sure to sell millions of books."

I find myself saying after brief reflection, "There are two kinds of 'great ideas' for books: One is the 'great idea' for a book with limited purchasing appeal. The other is a 'great idea' for a book that has *the potential to sell big*." Only the latter type interests me in almost all instances because I want to reach, interest, instruct, and help lots of people, and that means selling lots of books.

Diabetes can be the basis of many articles that sell well because you can provide some interesting information in limited space. For a book, the bottom line about diabetes has to be, "See a doctor and be guided routinely by the physician." Most people know that and won't pay the money for a book. There have been many worthy books on diabetes but none, within my knowledge, has sold big.

You must decide for yourself whether or not you wish to tackle a medical subject or other topic, even with prospects for only limited sale. But first, I emphasize again: *Investigate and make a sound marketing evaluation.* Then make a reasoned judgment.

When I was a beginner, my goal was primarily to get my books published, even with modest sales and payoff. I commend the same consideration to you: *Aim to get published.* Even now, after thirty published books, I'll write a book without best-seller possibilities if I want to enough for personal inner rewards. I turned down a big-money contract for a potential best-seller diet book to do this one now—because I care more about helping writers at this point than I do about earnings.

You'll make any such decisions for yourself—consciously.

PREPARE YOUR MIND PROCESS FOR SPARKING IDEAS

You'll positively increase your ability to come up with nonfiction ideas that sell by doing this: Start now to stimulate your natural mind processes systematically in the following ten simple, progressive ways-that-work. Many of these suggestions work for writing fiction, too.

The checklist that follows didn't originate from thin air. The cause-and-effect results overall have been double-checked and approved in studies and practical usage in varying forms. My own applications, and the experiences of a number of successful writers, educators, psychologists, and executives, confirm their effectiveness.

You'll benefit specifically and quickly when you check, intensify, and expand your mind processes through each of these thought-arousing boosts in turn. Just approach and study each step seriously and carefully now, and repeatedly in the future.

You can't miss as you follow through, applying and sharpening your basic abilities in successive stages 1-10, combining these elements with all the other ways-that-work provided in this book. These fundamentals have become the alphabet of success for many, including myself, who have absorbed and made them part of the idea-creating mind process in writing to sell.

For your own sake, please examine, analyze, and master these ten brief checkpoints not just as words and phrases. Each projects a vital facet of a successful system for finding salable writing ideas and subjects. *Realize that it is the LINKING of each and all of these essential elements that provides the strongest chain of accelerating and escalating thinking for productive and profitable idea conception.*

1.—Build your drive. Aspire more consciously to create ideas with true sales potential. The writer who is content with the first idea that pops is more likely to fail. You must constantly spur the desire to strive for *superior* topics, themes, concepts. Take a tip from chess champions whose commonly expressed credo is: "When you find the *perfect* move, look for a *better* one."

2.—Keep mentally "wide open." Persistently seek new approaches and possibilities, not limiting yourself to what is "usual" or generally "acceptable." Be alert and aware to note everything that happens to you and about you which might even possibly, however remotely, be useful in your writing. Maintain a *receptive, creative attitude* always. Otherwise, prime ideas may well be lost because your closed mind didn't observe and recognize them as potentially valuable for development.

As a youngster, I was reminded repeatedly of the necessity to be seeking and open. That prodding came from my creative-minded father, a textile manufacturer (creativity is not limited to writers). He stressed to me time after time that *no one becomes a fool until he stops asking questions.*

3.—Deepen your interest. Search always for the available power in creating possibilities for salable nonfiction from even fleeting happenings. You must dig beneath the surface in order to uncover writing gold. Example: A beginning writer told me that he'd heard someone comment at a cocktail party that he couldn't get any practical advice about how to handle his oncoming retirement. My friend was prompted to study the subject thoroughly. He has since sold many articles and a book on various aspects of retirement.

4.—Intensify multifaceted curiosity. Don't stop after considering an incident or possibility point-blank, upon looking briefly only at the obvious implication. Instead, attack the prospect from a multitude of aspects, from every searching direction: *Who? Why? When? Where? What if? How?* You'll be thrilled at the opportunities which had not been visible at first glance—when you look both with your open eyes and your mind's eye.

5.—*Cultivate thorough understanding.* Train yourself not only to investigate and understand ideas in depth but also to plumb all the parts that interlock to form the entity. The inevitable result of such thoroughness is that you won't skim over and lose a multitude of possibilities—either temporarily or permanently. Such negligence would result in opportunities lost. Instead, you'll discover many more promising openings leading to payoff ideas.

6.—*Focus your concentration sharply.* Train and keep your mind targeted to examine all details and routes to potential successful ideas. Never underestimate the power of concentration, a prime "secret of strength" in arriving at usable, rewarding conclusions that might otherwise be overlooked, never sighted, therefore lost totally.

7.—*Harness energy to thinking.* You can and should raise and maintain your energy level constantly and repeatedly in approaching, considering, and then bringing an appealing idea to fruition. Edison's assessment in this regard has become trite through overuse, but is nevertheless true that "genius is one percent inspiration and ninety-nine percent perspiration."

It's essential to keep exerting maximum vigor and drive in the pursuit of moneymaking ideas. In effect, you'll be exercising and thus building your mental muscles. Consider the encouraging fact that the "mind stretched by a new idea can never go back to its original dimension."

8.—*Strengthen your tenacity.* Make it part of your routine procedure in writing to keep coming back to a complex challenge time after time until you refine, simplify, and clarify the essence of an idea. Do this repeatedly, as much as necessary, to make the resultant manuscript readily understandable and thus more salable. Impatience has nullified many worthy possibilities in the early stages—which might have developed successfully if worked on sufficiently.

Be stubborn, persistent, steadfast in pursuing a promising subject to a productive conclusion. You'll get a double benefit: first, the gratification of overcoming a seemingly insurmountable obstacle, and second, ultimately making the sale.

9.—Elevate your enthusiasm. You'll find that eagerness combined with zeal and determined movement forward will raise both your ability and self-confidence. Working zestfully, you'll be giving every intriguing and developing idea the best possible chance to succeed. Clearheaded, objective optimism provides a far more promising starting point than being pessimistic and therefore negative.

A doctor friend referred to optimism one day, in speaking of a seriously ailing patient, as a "healthy heart stimulant." I added that sound optimism, for a determined writer, is a mind stimulation, too. You can get this valuable stimulant free through concentration and application, not from a chemist shop.

10.—Maintain a cooperative attitude. Always consider and weigh rationally the reactions and suggestions of others. Such recommendations will often lead to your making modifications and additions that can render a previously fuzzy or weak idea practical and profitable. I've found repeatedly that being cooperative with editors and others has sparked some of my most successful writing accomplishments. In short, be receptive, not automatically negative in your reactions.

Summing up, utilize the ten elements habitually. Now . . . please reread, study, and practice every one of the preceding ten approaches to creating better, more acceptable ideas. Make them part of the natural, most efficient and effective functioning of your personal mind processes. Nurture all these elements as your own:

> *drive ... openness ... interest ... curiosity ... understanding ... enthusiasm ... cooperation ... concentration ... energy ... tenacity.*

There you have them to adopt and apply from now on—the ten links in the chain that leads to more and more effective ideas as you make increasing amounts of money from writing.

P.S. These ten fundamentals are not only basic elements from which profitable writing ideas grow, but also from which conscious happiness and maximum daily rewards from living develop and flourish.

THE SUBJECT SHOULD INTEREST YOU . . . IN ORDER TO INTEREST OTHERS BEST

If a subject strikes you as dull and even boring, but you decide to tackle it because you think it will interest lots of readers, you're *not* likely to sell the piece. A writer's lack of enthusiasm usually comes through in the finished article. Most editors can feel that immediately. They'll reject the offering and usually lose some respect for the writer.

Instead, turn your attention and energy to the multitudes of topics that interest *you* as well as many readers. If a subject excites you, then you can convey that electricity most interestingly and informatively in your writing. You'll *enjoy* the writing, as you should, and you'll better the chance that others will enjoy the reading.

BECOME INTERESTED TO BE MORE INTERESTING

Earlier, you were warned not to write about a subject if you find it dull—because that lack of interest will come through in the written piece. Here's a different slant, how a seemingly dull topic can often become interesting to you and editors and readers: Before you reject a subject out of hand, it often pays to *probe be-*

neath the surface first. Usually, you'll discover hidden facts and facets, dramatic details that will involve and help readers.

Example: Internationally noted psychoanalyst Dr. Leopold Bellak approached me and suggested that we write a book on *physiognomy,* in which he is expert. My first reaction was silently negative . . . "Who cares about physiognomy?" He proposed that I think about it and left me some material from medical journals to study. Because I respected him highly, I agreed—but unenthusiastically.

The dictionary describes physiognomy—"the face as an index to character." I still wasn't impressed but decided to look into the possibilities. I dug in and soon understood that while a book *about physiognomy* seemed uninviting, teaching people *how to read faces* for many personal benefits would have a good chance of exciting individuals—and therefore publishers.

Now *I* became stimulated and put together a presentation (the "how" will be told later). The first publisher to see the presentation for *Reading Faces* (Dr. Bellak's title) went for it. The book generated a hardcover, paperback, magazine excerpts, the works.

The cogent lessons here are threefold: First . . . if I'd stopped at my instant negative reaction, without investigating diligently, I'd have overlooked the possibilities. Second . . . if projected to publishers as a book "about physiognomy," it probably would have been rejected. Third . . . clear, simple, illuminating writing had to convey specific reader self-benefit—and prove it.

Without question, you must become involved and enthusiastic before you can arouse needed enthusiasm in publishers, editors, and readers. You must examine the proposition in depth. Then, if you can't convey solid evidence of stimulation and benefit in your sample chapters and total presentation, you're not likely to make the sale.

It comes down to this always: When you write to sell, an essential requisite for all subjects is to capture *reader interest.* Never lose sight of that. Be analytical, involved, enthusiastic about whatever you write about—and convey that spirit. You'll be more successful not only at writing but also—and more important—at living.

HOW TO MAKE A COMMON
SUBJECT SALABLE

Don't be turned off a subject because you're not an expert on that topic. Instead, *become an expert*. Dig in, study published articles, analyze available research, set up your own "research" by getting in touch with and interviewing authorities. *Work at it*. If you don't, you won't be a selling writer—and you're going to be, or I will have written this book in vain.

Devise creative approaches that illuminate the subject in a more understandable, more usable, more resultful way. No topic is just one subject—each offers hundreds, thousands of angles for the resourceful, inventive writer. These slants grow from digging into, nurturing, and expanding the information you amass.

Let's consider "diet" as an example of one subject offering endless possibilities. I've sold varied diet articles on "New 14-Day Shape-Up" . . . "Speedy Summer Diet" . . . "Three-Day Quickie Diet" . . . "Before-and-After Holiday Diet" . . . "Pre-Summer Swimsuit Diet" . . . "Computer Diet," the first in that category, latching quickly onto new technology . . . the list goes on and on and on.

Get the point? You're limited only by yourself if you allow yourself to think that everything has been said and written before on *any* subject. Banish that thought for all time. I assure you that if you plant the seeds in your mind—sound facts, pertinent basic information, and proved knowledge—*new ideas will grow* which you can transform into salable writing, no matter how common the subject.

DISDAIN THE VOICE OF
DOOM: "IT'S BEEN DONE
BEFORE"

More writers have dropped ideas that could have sold because a well-meaning friend or "expert" has said, "Don't try that subject, it's been done before." I must impress this upon you forcefully again: *"Much of my writing success has been based on doing DIFFERENTLY what 'has been done before'!"*

When I was beginning, an editor told me flatly, "We're not interested in diet pieces, the subject has been overdone—forget it." A few years later, after my diet best-seller achievements, she apologized: "I didn't realize that you'd make an overdone subject new and fresh and exceptionally helpful." She added, "How about doing a diet article for us?" I did a number of them.

Let this buoy you up always: There are countless ways for you to write and sell what's been done before. Study offshoot slants, work out ingenious creative twists that will make the subject come through as something *new* and *different*, and emphasize the *difference in approach* when you query editors. Selling writers do that every day. Try it, work at it, and you can't help but succeed.

Just don't be afraid to venture because doomsayers erect unsound barriers. Derive inspiration and impetus from the words of a creative genius, Dr. Edward Land, inventor of the Polaroid camera. His statement has emboldened me for years: *"An essential aspect of creativity is not being afraid to fail."*

Don't Fear Competition, Follow Your Convictions

Many others involved with writing won't agree with this, but I pass on to you the *fact* that I've profited by seldom fearing competition. I suggest that you do the same. Too many aspiring writers have been put off a subject because they're told, "It's been done before." If you are convinced that you have something particularly fresh, valuable, and helpful to say to readers, go to it.

When I was writing my first diet book, another successful editor of a leading women's magazine warned me emphatically (because she had my interests in mind), "Samm, stop writing your diet book—save yourself wasted time and energy. I've just bought prepublication rights for a roundup diet book which provides over one hundred diets of every type. It will kill the chances of your diet book and any others for now."

I believed in the book, wrote it, endured sixteen rejections until the seventeenth publisher okayed it reluctantly at the insistence of an ardent, determined editor (sure, editors differ, too). It scored as *The Doctor's Quick Weight Loss Diet,* the #2 best-selling diet book of all time. (Incidentally, the "roundup" book flopped; my editor friend bought me an expensive lunch to apologize: "It isn't the last mistake I'll make.")

The significant lesson here is that if others try to discourage you from writing on a subject you believe in, do this: Reexamine your project from every angle—the market, the potential. Then, I repeat, *if you are convinced that you have something fresh, some especially worthwhile aid to convey to readers,* damn the competition and go ahead.

Good fortune to you—you will have earned it.

Uncover the Unique Perspective That Sells

If you have something special to contribute, no matter how "overwritten" the subject may seem to be, you can still write and sell by approaching the overall topic this way: Project *your* particular expertise or exceptional perspective. Here's how this applies, exemplified by one of the most published categories of all—*cookbooks.*

Instead of the defeatist attitude that "there's nothing new under the sun," discover that outstanding "something new," as successful writers do. On my desk is an issue of *Publishers Weekly,* "The Journal of the Book Industry" (a very valuable publication you'll probably find at your public library, since head librarians read it unfailingly). The section reviewing oncoming books, "PW Forecasts," includes these cookbooks:

- *The I'm Sick of Carrot Sticks Cookbook*
- *The Book for Great Soups, Sandwiches, and Breads*
- *Classic Italian Cooking for the Vegetarian Gourmet*
- *The Gourmet and Gourmand Cajun Cookbook*
- *The Southern Pies and Pastry Cookbook*
- *The Pizza Book: The World's Greatest Pie*

At a painting workshop, a proud husband said, "My wife makes the best appetizers and snacks in the world." The beginning writer wrote *The Before and After Dinner Cook Book,* published by Atheneum. The first book of an alert gentleman who didn't cook is *The Best of the Best,* "Recipes from America's top restaurants, famous chefs and good cooks I've known," published by Quadrangle/Times Books.

Another enterprising author cashed in with a twofold twist: *The Supermarket Cookbook AND Shopping Guide,* published by Simon & Schuster. The lesson is clear, no matter what the writing category: Look for and uncover the special slant. Thus you can sell, no matter how competitive the field may be.

Don't be Scared Off
or Stymied by Competition

A letter in the mail today from a clergyman-writer presented a very intelligent proposal, including a detailed outline, for a book he wanted me to coauthor. (I turned him down gently because (a) I'm concentrating on my own books, and (b) the subject wouldn't excite me even if I had time and if all the other basics for coauthorship were resolved.)

What bothered me, and makes a vital point for you, is that his letter went into detail about extensive research into whether the subject had been covered in articles or books recently. I sensed great indecision and fear, along with what I consider a waste of time. Just think of this—if everyone worried about the competition . . .

- ... nobody would ever write again about diet or sex or exercise or cooking or controversy or hundreds of other popular topics . . .
- ... everyone would be stymied by concern that "it's been done before."

Of course, practically each important subject has been "done before" since the first word was written, because these primary topics interest most people. Why inhibit your subject choice because similar themes have appeared in published articles or books, as listed in reference guides? How do you know that comparable items are not being printed right now, but haven't been recorded yet?

My advice is to proceed if the subject excites you . . . and will stimulate, inform, and help potential readers. *Just offer something better, more valuable, a fresh creative twist.* Countless times one editor says, "No, old stuff"—and the next cheers, "Terrific, just what we want!"

Don't be afraid to venture, to dare, to break the mold. Have the courage to strive, perhaps to fail . . . *or to succeed.*

CONSIDER SPECIALIZING IN SELECTED SUBJECTS

This is important for you to study, whether your efforts are being bought and published now, or inevitably will be published in the future, as long as you keep writing enough. Many writers are losing out on their highest earning capacity from their work by jumping too quickly from subject to subject. They simply don't give enough thought to the marketing possibilities in each.

I urge you to mull over the gains that can accrue for you in narrowing your choices and specializing in one topic after another in depth. In probing each theme in turn most deeply, you can sell and gain the utmost, far more than many writers realize. There are two simple, basic questions to answer for yourself in choosing each subject on which to concentrate:

One: Does the subject interest *me* enough to give it a good deal of time, attention, and effort?

Two: Does the subject have enough interest and appeal for *editors and readers* to warrant the dedication and work that are necessary?

If you answer yes to both questions, then plan and follow through on one selected subject after another. Then you'll make the most of the publishing and earning opportunities in each.

A definite bonus from such specialization is that you will become an authority in each subject. Accordingly, your writing will have increasing appeal for editors and readers. In many instances, editors will approach you to write an article on that topic as it fits in with their current needs.

You'll usually find that as you dig deeper into each subject, you don't become bored. Rather, as you expand your knowledge of the topic, exciting and stimulating new angles will appear for you to investigate and convey to readers.

Just be certain that you select subjects with a sufficient audience and market, large or small. Of course, the larger the readership, the greater the money payoff. The primary consideration, however, in my mind and experience, is *to be published*, to sell and keep selling. The gains will grow, as demonstrated.

GROW MULTIPLE SALES FROM ONE BASIC IDEA

When you're good at some pursuit, such as gardening, sewing, teaching . . . or have a special interest, perhaps sports, pets . . . consider concentrating on ideas about that subject. Then, when you sell a piece, *multiply sales through various ideas on that same topic*. Many successful examples support that point:

- A beginning writer, who also happened to be a home gardener, finally sold a piece to a gardening magazine. Instead of scattering his shots, he kept aiming at the same target. A book followed, a radio series on gardening, on and on.
- A woman who sewed a great deal, and was striving to be a writer, unexpectedly sold a how-to crocheting article to the local newspaper. The home-page editor asked for more. Now she augments her family income by writing about sewing and other subjects.
- An educator who tried writing about other matters was invited to be the expert in coauthoring a book of advice to parents of schoolchildren. She quit as a school head and is busy writing in that category.
- A pet lover and aspiring writer followed up a local radio interview on the care of cats and dogs with one article, then successive slants.
- A successful writer on sports failed to sell anything on a va-

riety of subjects; finally, he scored with an interview of a football star, took off from there.

Variety can certainly be the spice of writing life, but you can successfully combine diversity *and* specialization. Like other authors, I've accomplished that with five gardening books, seven diet books, many books and articles on health and fitness. Don't bypass the dual possibilities for *your* writing career.

Chapter Four

MORE MONEY-MAKING IDEAS YOU NEVER HAD ANY IDEA ABOUT BEFORE

A brilliant gentleman who has scored as one of the most creative and successful textile designers complained some years back to my father, with whom he worked, "Each season I present a line of dozens of original new designs. Within a few weeks, they've been knocked off, copied, and offered to stores by competitors at lower prices. It's killing me that others steal my creative ideas!"

The experienced older man advised, "Don't waste your time and talent worrying about that. Just keep digging for new ideas, creating new designs and fabrics. There's no ceiling, no limit on ideas." The designer absorbed and applied the sage counsel. He has become more wealthy and successful than he had thought possible.

The same thinking is true for writing. Here are more ideas to stimulate your innovative thinking and doing. Follow through energetically and industriously, and you can't help but make money writing. Each worthy idea you originate and put into practice will sprout dozens more that pay off.

It has been noted and proved that a person's mind, expanded by a creative new idea, will never go back to its former lesser dimension. Each well-reasoned idea you create will be just the start of many more of increasing value for you.

SIX STEPS TO MAKE A
SUBJECT G-R-O-W

It has aided me immeasurably in practically all my writing for a variety of media, print and otherwise, to help a subject sprout and flourish in six successive steps. I printed the stages large on a card some time ago, which I refer to often when I start a new writing project. The six simple steps (perhaps stemming from my garden writing experience) are disclosed here for the first time anywhere:

1. Start with the seed idea . . . You have the idea you want to write about—based on something in your background perhaps, or perhaps the many recommendations in this book for getting ideas. Now you have the seed.

2. Plant the seed in your mind . . . Examine the quality of the seed: Is there a market for this subject? Are the possibilities good for selling the idea once written? If your answers are yes, then push the seed deep into your unconscious/subconscious mind, leaving it there to germinate and to feed you needed answers when required, as will be explained in the next segment in the book. Go on to the next steps.

3. Fertilize and cultivate the seed . . . Seek out facts, research, essential findings relating to your subject and idea. Write them down. Study the data. Fill your mind with all you've learned about the topic.

4. Make the plant grow by writing your first draft . . . Start writing, keep writing, until you have the entire manuscript down on paper or on word processor disks, in rough form.

5. Cultivate further and shape the plant by rewriting . . . Go back over your pages, or on the computer screen or printout, right from start to finish. Clarify. Revise. Cut. Add. Delve into and "command" your unconscious mind to come up with answers and improvements; this process will be described shortly.

6. Offer your final "money plant" (article) or "money tree" (book manuscript) . . . At last you're satisfied that you have the fully grown article or book manuscript to offer. Check again to be sure you present it to the best markets, publications, publishers. This is a fundamental way that works more surely, speedily, and inevitably than a disorganized *modus operandi*.

USE YOUR UNCONSCIOUS/ SUBCONSCIOUS MIND . . . AN UNLIMITED "FREE" RESOURCE

Try this thought-process "miracle" that works for me and many others I've instructed. When I need an idea or a further advance in writing, and it doesn't come readily, I think deeply about the problem for a few minutes in bed in the dark just before sleeping. (Nothing mystic about this, you're simply using your natural mind processes more efficiently.) Then I "command" my mind optimistically, "Come up with a solution by the time I awaken." And off to sleep . . .

Usually (not always, so I try the next night if I can't find the answers consciously), I awaken at some hour with the needed solution. Example: Yesterday I lunched with a top professional writer of short stories, novels, exceptional juvenile books, and some nonfiction. She said she had used this unconscious mind system successfully the previous night.

"I finished my latest book a few weeks ago. My editor called, said she loved the manuscript, but rejected the title. I submitted some new titles, and she offered some, but not one suited us both. She pressured me, so I told myself before sleep last night, 'Wake up with the perfect title!' Incredible—I awakened at 3:00 A.M. with a six-word title, wrote it down, *perfect*. Phoned editor next morning, she okayed it enthusiastically."

Sound unbelievable? Try it—find out for yourself.

You must put facts in before solutions can emerge. You can't get the right, usable ideas and answers out of your mind and into salable writing until you devote needed study, research, and a great deal of thinking. Material you can utilize effectively rarely emerges from an *empty* mind.

You may have experienced this, as so many have related with great excitement: "I was shaving (or powdering my nose)—not even thinking consciously about a complicated problem that had baffled me for months. Then suddenly the answer popped out—a miracle." Now you know that it wasn't an accident, just evidence of the unconscious mind at work.

Again, don't just dream and hope——DO!

Don't fail to write down the solution. I keep a little pad, a pen, and a pen-size flashlight by my bed so that if I awaken with an idea or answer or reminder, I write it down. It's sometimes hard to decipher the "sleepwriting," but I manage. If you don't do likewise already, I advise it strongly.

A common instance is that of a scientist who labored for many months to complete a chemical formula, but one vital element eluded him. He studied, strained, couldn't capture the baffling connection. One night he awakened with the answer displayed on a TV screen in his head. "Eureka!" he shouted, and returned to sleep. When he awoke, his mind was a blank. It took him months more to arrive at the solution.

Write it down.

More proof of how this practice works. The remarkable processing in the unconscious mind has been substantiated repeatedly by professionally conducted tests like this: You are taken into a furnished room unfamiliar to you. After an aimless chat of five minutes or so, you go to another room. You are asked to list in writing, without pausing, all the objects you recall having seen in the first room. You may note about twenty objects.

You are then hypnotized. Under hypnosis, you're asked to list the objects you saw in the first room. In many such tests, the person listed as many as *two hundred* or more items. The unconscious mind was busy gathering information at an amazingly fast rate, far more speedily than the conscious mind.

Don't overlook using this priceless writing resource.

WRITE DOWN THE
THOUGHT . . . OR LOSE IT

If you are really a writer or a writer-to-be (if not, you wouldn't be reading this how-to book), then some fraction of your mind is always looking for and discovering potential writing/selling ideas. As happens with me (and for you), when reading a newspaper, magazine, book, listening to radio, watching TV, whatever I'm doing, my mind is alert to seeking and finding ideas for my writing projects.

Filling a diary or notebook later is helpful, but writing a quick note *immediately*, if only a few indicative words, keeps ideas from fading and vanishing.

That's why I emphasize that it's not only desirable but necessary that you write down the thought instantly on a slip of paper!

If you don't write the idea or the "tickle" or the possibility down on paper, you'll probably lose it—certainly for now, perhaps forever. A pencil or pen and a small pad are present in my shirt pocket, or other pocket, *always*—I feel naked without them. You don't value your mind enough if you don't immediately record what your thought processes spew out. (If you haven't a pad, tear a bit of paper from the newspaper or a magazine and make the note on that.)

Don't be self-conscious about this. As a selling writer, you can't afford to be embarrassed. Many times, in the midst of a conversation with someone or with a group, I'll grab my pen and tiny pad and write down the thought just sparked. Sure, people look at me with that expression—"What kind of a nut is he?" Doesn't bother me, shouldn't faze you: *I'm a writing nut, the kind of nut I want to be; so are you.*

This book contains many tips sparked by just such out-of-nowhere thoughts. This recommendation, for example, zoomed in while reading a newspaper report on the geyser Old Faithful. I'm puzzled by what the connection might be, but the fact is that the thought spurted through my mind, I jotted it down, and here it is. May seem weird, but the jot-it-now system works—my writing earnings prove it. Your increased income will convince you, too.

Jot a "Tomorrow Memo" for Yourself

When I finish writing for the day, I always jot down in the margin, or at bottom of the page, or on a separate sheet—*what comes next.* Such as: "Tell about the importance of weighing yourself daily." Or: "Give details of the proper breathing exercises." If fiction: "Clark sets out for the champagne area and meeting with bureau heads."

This what-comes-next notation serves two prime purposes: (1) it relieves my mind of worrying about how I'll start writing the next morning; and (2) the details develop in my unconscious mind overnight and provide a springboard to speedy writing action to start the new day.

PICK YOUR BEST TIME FOR DEVELOPING IDEAS

You may benefit greatly, as many writers have, from surveying and selecting your best time and place for creating ideas and writing. That depends entirely on your personal situation and needs, for—like everything in this book—the emphasis is on your *individuality*. Nothing suggests in the slightest degree that you ever *conform* to a narrow, confined mold or model.

As one with a demanding full-time job plus overtime, striving to advance in a business career, I trained myself—of necessity—to write at just about any time and in any place. Nevertheless, writing at a certain time of day or night works best for some successful authors, and may for you, since every person's mind works on a different time-efficiency basis.

The vital point here is that all the ways-that-work are to help *you* write to sell, not me. If you'll study and work with them, as they may fit you, then they must and will work for you. Perhaps one of the following examples will illuminate how you can write best in accordance with your own daily schedule:

Harriet, a selling free-lance writer, has a nine-to-five job as an executive secretary. She races from the office to the supermarket most days, then prepares dinner for her husband and three kids (I'm not justifying this family's routine, I'm simply reporting). After the others have gone to bed, Harriet hits her typewriter from 10:00 P.M. to midnight. She told me, "I've been packing my writing into those two hours daily for several years now. I can't concentrate at other times, but I fill a lot of pages just about every weekday night."

Walter, an important writer who turns out a book a year, along with articles and other writing that sells, has fitted time to his internal clock. An early riser, he has maintained a rigid writing schedule for years—whether home, vacationing, or on business and promotional travels. He writes from six to eleven each morning, including Saturdays and Sundays. His alarm goes off at eleven, and he stops, even in the middle of a sentence. He says, "My mental energy starts to diminish at that hour, and I'll write only at my best." Inflexible? It works for him.

Cynthia writes from 9:00 to 11:30 A.M. weekdays. She explains, "I established that routine when my kids went off to school. At nine sharp, I turn off the phone and ignore the doorbell. I squat at my desk and *write*, quitting in time to get lunch ready. My relatives, friends, and neighbors know that *nothing* is permitted to interrupt, or I'd never be a selling writer."

What's your best creative time period for originating ideas and making them pay off through words? Consider that carefully. Otherwise, time may creep away in its steady pace from day to day, with little accomplished. Pinning down a specific time to write may be a crucial aid for you.

SET YOUR THEME . . . THEN FOLLOW THROUGH

To write to sell, it's essential to pinpoint your subject and theme for an article or book. Then carry through your basic premise to the conclusion, without deviating and losing your reader's attention, interest, and belief. Taking side roads off the main throughway can transform a likely sale into a failure.

Precise example: When I left Madison Avenue, I wrote a book manuscript, *The Permissible Lie: The Inside Truth About Advertising*. This exposé named hundreds of specific campaigns which were deceiving, misleading, and demeaning to the public. I concluded each chapter with some ads which succeeded without lying, proof that advertisers could sell without falsifications and putdowns.

After a rejection, my agent phoned: "A smart editor said the theme is sidetracked and weakened fatally by the repeated intrusion of the apologetic examples. You should combine them all in one concluding chapter." I made the change. The published book was a notable success. *I urge you to avoid my mistake.*

Historic sidelight: In spite of the revision, sixteen rejections followed as editors admitted typically, "Too controversial. Powerful advertising interests might cause trouble." The seventeenth editor approved courageously. As finished books were being shipped, the dominant magazine conglomerate which owned the book publisher suppressed the book. A media explosion erupted as the *New York Times* and publications worldwide reported "the first such censorship in book publishing history." Rights were returned to me; another publisher grabbed the book, which, due to the shocking publicity, became a bigger seller than it probably would have before the controversy.

LIST MANY IDEAS . . .
THEN MAKE THEM PAY

To avoid getting stymied, *don't stop with one idea!* Set yourself down and don't get up until you list a dozen or more ideas on your selected subject. That always pays out for me. I keep writing varied slants, sensible or screwball. Then I pick the most promising twist and proceed with that for an article (that may grow into a book). It works as simply as this:

1. Select a subject that promises a reading audience.
2. List up to a dozen or more idea variations.

3. Pick the one idea that's most promising.
4. *Start to write* determinedly, persistently—perhaps slowly at first, then you pick up steam and roll along.
5. Reread, revise, to clarify for potential readers.
6. Submit the piece for publication. Immediately repeat the entire process. And again—again—and again. Do that . . . and you just can't help but write *and* sell.

DON'T PASS UP IDEAS FROM YOUR OWN BACKGROUND

A woman in a writing class handed me a few of her pieces that had been rejected. At the next session, I said, "These articles are about high society, but they don't ring true [clearly, she wasn't a jet-setter]. Maybe you'd write more convincingly about what you know well. What's your work?"

"Dull," she explained. "I'm a clerk in a drugstore. Nothing interesting happens."

"No?" I challenged, "Don't you get any weird requests? Wacky complaints? Oddball customers? Any break-ins?"

As she answered, ideas started popping as we chuckled over far-out customer gripes, anecdotes about doctor prescriptions. "Write them up!" I urged. She nodded enthusiastically. Sold the article to the first magazine on her list.

Others in the adult education class drew from their own backgrounds: A textile worker wrote a fascinating piece following raw materials step by step from the loom to a stunning gown on a fashion model. A mailman strung together hilarious happenings on his route. A teacher related how one of her brightest students turned on with drugs—but ultimately was saved.

A number of these beginning writers started collecting checks instead of rejections. Certainly you can write on almost any idea by filling out with research, interviews, other probing. Go ahead . . . but don't overlook rewards from your own hard-earned experience. Intimate knowledge often packs idea and writing power.

PULL SALABLE IDEAS
FROM DAILY HAPPENINGS

It's strange but true: Many would-be writers, seeking salable ideas frantically, often pass up what's under their noses. They consider such subjects "uninteresting."

Chatting at a writing seminar, an attractive young woman said, "I told my mother that my doctor had noted a skin cancer on my cheek, was going to remove it. She fainted. When she revived, I assured her that the condition was curable. But when I repeated 'skin cancer,' she collapsed again."

I said, "Great idea for an article on skin cancer." Blank faces. I persisted, "Most people fear skin cancer because they're ignorant about it. The reassuring facts should be told. Anybody want to write about it?" Negative shrugs.

Next day I sent a query letter to a national magazine, repeating the incident verbatim. Green light. I cashed in with a piece, "Foiling Skin Cancer." An amazed member of the group commented, "Gosh, you're lucky!"

At another session, we discussed capital punishment. A doctor made a dramatic point from his personal experience. "That's an article idea," I suggested. The others reacted, "It's no use." I wrote it up, added similar case histories, sold the piece.

An English instructor told of meeting the dean of a progressive preparatory school who mentioned some new theories he was trying. When I suggested she write it up, she said, "It's old stuff." Old to her, new to the public. I used it for an article, "The High School of the Future," pocketed the check.

Keep a constant "listening ear" for ideas . . . When you hear something intriguing at a dinner party or when chatting with neighbors, for instance, do you simply comment like others, "That's fascinating"? Or do you make a note and follow up for future writing? Proceeding further, instead of doing nothing, can make a dollars-and-cents difference when you write to sell.

At a Saturday night gathering, a woman from New York City mentioned her work as a volunteer for a group known as "English in Action." She described how she and others helped foreign visitors who couldn't speak or understand English. As "goodwill ambassadors," members guided and interpreted for travelers, who later returned home enthusiastic about America and Americans.

All present complimented her, then turned to other subjects. I said that I was a writer and saw article possibilities. Eager for publicity, she sent me literature. Using the material, I followed up with interviews, wrote an article which I sold to a national women's magazine, plus three additional pieces I later sold elsewhere.

Too often, writers overlook ideas sprouting underfoot because they're focusing too far out. Ideas are occurring all about you. Open your eyes and ears, see, listen, investigate, write, and profit.

I was invited to one of the monthly dinner meetings of a society of magazine writers in another city. Through the hours of conversation at our round table, I noted the staring, acquisitive eyes questioning: "Is there a salable idea for *me* in what she or he is saying?" I deplored the competitive pressure, but these professionals were working constantly, *on the hunt for ideas.*

CASH IN QUICKLY ON "LUCK" . . . OR LOSE OUT

Every writer must follow through immediately when Lady Luck opens a door—or else opportunities for rewards tend to disappear. Example:

Reading the *New York Times Magazine,* I found that a line in an article on beauty care caught my eye. Dumb luck, I guess, since I wasn't interested in the subject at the time. I read something about the smart people of Scarsdale becoming skinny, thanks to a diet sheet available from a Dr. Tarnower. I sent a stamped, self-addressed envelope for a copy.

At a Writers' Lunch Seminar, I told how I'd then written at once to Dr. Herman Tarnower about possible coauthorship. A meeting and agreement resulted in the blockbuster best-seller. A listening writer screamed, "My God, I read that article. I could have contacted Dr. Tarnower and had a best-seller!" She groaned, "Some people have all the luck. . . ."

The secret to cashing in on "luck" is to sight and *do* something positive instantly about an opening. In another instance, a publisher—impressed by my gardening ad writing—suggested that I consider offering a garden book proposal. Natalie asked, "Isn't that too much work, involving overwhelming, time-consuming detail—on a gamble?" Tempted to goof off, instead I created a definitive presentation which clicked and led to my five very successful gardening books. Clearly, *luck* must be teamed with *labor.*

Luck also introduced me to Dr. Irwin Stillman's daughter-in-law at a Westchester dinner party. She'd heard about my doctor-coauthored skin problems book, and talked me into a lunch date next day with Dr. Stillman in New York City, an hour away. A blizzard developed overnight. Tempted to forget the whole idea, instead I left home at dawn, fought the storm, kept the date. Result—a "lucky" blockbuster.

Think about it: How many opportunities have you lost because you missed the turn after luck pointed the way? You have to *look* for luck . . . *recognize* the possibility . . . *follow through* industriously. That's nourishing food for thought (not necessarily diet food). Prepare your mind now to seize the chance instantly when "luck" beckons. Longfellow agrees: "Do not delay: the golden moments fly!"

SEIZE THE IDEA THAT CAN SKYROCKET YOUR CAREER

Are you overlooking ideas that can skyrocket your career, like the following example? The right action may make a wonderful lifelong difference for you, as it did for me.

Waiting on a commuter train platform, I overheard two men in their sixties chatting. One said, "I told you I was going to expand my business, but I doubt whether I'm up to it. *I'm not as young as I used to be.*"

Without thinking, I turned and said, "You never were!

You've never been as young as you used to be. On your ninth birthday, you weren't as young as you used to be at eight, one day before. So why discourage yourself with those gloomy words, 'I'm not as young as I used to be'? You never were; why let the thought drag you down now?"

The train arrived, and we separated. Months later, I ran into the same man. He grabbed my hand and said, "Thanks for telling me off that day at the train. It changed my outlook. I went ahead with my business expansion and it's going great. Y'know ... *I'm much younger than I used to be.*"

When I related that story, the response was so enthusiastic that I wrote it up. Mailed it to one of the leading publications then (1962), *This Week* newspaper magazine, which had over 14 million circulation. Back came a check with an uplifting letter from the editor, stating that my piece would run as a featured full page; they wanted more submissions. *My first mass-circulation magazine sale!*

I was on my way. Ever since, I've transformed small encounters like this into articles that sold. But if I'd simply regarded them as "a funny thing happened on the train platform" and elsewhere, as most people do, I'd have missed a multitude of writing/selling gains. How about you?

Think twice when something occurs—then *write it up*.

DIG IDEAS OUT OF NEWSPAPERS, NEWSMAGAZINES

Don't overlook this source: Just one newspaper on one day yielded the following potential payoff ideas from headlines and opening lines of news stories:

- Clues to improved hospital quality and sizable medical-care savings the public should know about.
- Small-city mayor proves it possible to provide better services and lower tax costs.
- New treatments used in clinics prevent many common illness flare-ups.

- In home tests, air-conditioning costs cut one-fourth by these few simple rules.
- A new model state program cuts insurance fees up to 20 percent for homeowners.
- Important clinical tests show back troubles reduced drastically through proper chair design.
- Women's campaign reduces local pornography in movies and TV programs in simple ways that could be adapted by other communities.

Newsmagazines also are teeming with ideas for salable articles. In my file is a report I clipped recently about a young woman lawyer who risked her career and reputation to help her lover, a convicted killer she had defended, to escape from prison. They were captured later. I wrote on the clipping: "Terrific idea for a nonfiction crime article." Subjects of all kinds are just waiting to be written about profitably.

Yes, your newspapers and newsmagazines are filled with article ideas as good as or better than these for expanding into pieces that sell. Do this:

1. Select subjects that interest you most.
2. Research material and expand into article size.
3. Offer your articles to the right magazine or newspaper-supplement markets.

CULL IDEAS FROM REPUTABLE NEWS RELEASES

"Story Ideas" is a monthly public relations sheet mailed to freelance writers, publications, and others by Carnegie-Mellon University. The release offers data and information from experts at the university. Personal interviews with them will be arranged if you desire. One listing I received covers detailed investigative material on these diverse subjects:

- Advanced computer enlightenment for nontechnical college students.
- Updated training in managerial skills for government employees.
- More electrical power from computer-controlled solar systems.
- How Japan's economy has grown through technological innovation.
- How the new global economy dictates the rules of the economic game worldwide now and for the future.

Similar help for writers seeking ideas and information in depth is offered by monthly or periodic mailings which include:

- "Leads . . . from the University of Iowa Health Center"
- "News . . . from University of Texas Science Center at Dallas"
- "Health Update from the American Hospital Association"
- "Newstips from Upjohn Company for science journalists"
- "Turnaround Times from Campbell's Institute for Health and Fitness"
- "Georgetown University News" (primarily health developments)
- "People For The AMERICAN WAY, Citizens for Constitutional Concerns"
- "News from Alan Guttmacher Institute of Research, Policy Analysis and Public Education"

I've sent for and obtained valuable information from the offered printed data, phone and in-person interviews, through the various, eager public relations departments. Such material has helped me write and sell published articles and books. You can benefit similarly.

The preceding names are just a very few of the many that offer considerable new information on research and developments in many fields. Look up listings in the directories available at your public library. Write to them, asking to be placed on their mailing lists. You'll be provided month after month with ideas and sources for additional in-depth material.

GET IDEAS VIA LISTINGS IN WRITER DIRECTORIES

As a writer, getting your name listed in leading directories such as *Working Press of the Nation* brings a lot of publicity material from commercial companies. Many of the releases are simply self-serving ballyhoo of little or no use. Nevertheless, I've derived valuable ideas, data, and invitations to meetings where I've heard experts present details on fascinating research and advances. These have led to profitable contacts and published manuscripts.

Your listing, which you supply, will show subjects of particular interest to you as a writer. Topics following my name include: advertising, art, business, diet, economics, gardening, government, health, psychology, science, sex, sociology.

You'll receive so many mailings that examination will occupy a little time almost daily separating the useful from the waste matter. I glean enough benefit to make the inspection worthwhile for me. A recent mail brought a fascinating, hilarious sample of a Giant Six-Foot Scarecrow Snake, along with information about a Realistic Scarecrow Great Horned Owl.

I read the details, blew up the vinyl Giant Six-Foot Scarecrow Snake, placed it in our garden. Next morning I found a deceased raccoon, scared to death by the monstrous snake (no, no, that's a joke, ma'am). Literature provides reports from respected universities, use of the air-filled snakes at the White House (naturally), all sorts of factual goodies.

Silly? Not when I bet that I could sell one or more pieces on this provocative item, factual or humorous. You could, too, applying your personal curiosity and creativity. So get listed in the right directories. Then mine the mails for usable, moneymaking writing ideas. Look up such directories or get a listing of them at your public library. Follow through as you see fit; have a sharp letter-opener handy.

SEEK OFFSHOOT IDEAS AS YOU READ, SEE, HEAR

Be alert to create your own writing/selling ideas that can spring from what you read daily, see on TV and elsewhere, hear on radio and other communications outlets. Note these three specific illustrations of how you can evolve tangential inspirations and then cash in.

Bill W., a young writer seeking a break, remarked that he was sick of getting rejections. I said, "The subjects you say you've offered don't seem to me to convey much excitement." In talking generally, he expressed enthusiasm about a rock music star, "but I read in an article about him that his sexual habits are questionable." I suggested, "There's an offshoot idea—how about an article on the sexual attitudes of today's young music stars?" Bill grabbed the subject, conducted a batch of interviews, sold the piece.

Carol T., at a writer's gathering, explained that she'd been reading a question-and-answer article in a magazine about tax problems: "Suddenly it hit me—my kids' pediatrician said on our last visit that he'd like to coauthor a piece with me on youngsters' primary health problems. So how about a question-and-answer format? That unlocked the direction for me. I wrote it up and the article will be published in two months."

Barbara W., attending a writing class, said, "I've just made my first sale. The idea came out of left field. I was watching a fine chef's demonstration on TV. He told the interviewer that he'd started years back by attending a cooking course given by a woman in her home. I thought, 'Hey, how about a roundup giving details of cooking classes in the area?' I went ahead, sold the piece to a newspaper Sunday supplement last week."

There you are: Play the angles. Always keep your mind aware and open for writing possibilities that slant off from what's happening each minute. Appetizing ideas are cooking everywhere. It's up to you to sniff them out, write them up, make the sale. Nobody else is going to do that for you—it's all part of the special excitement and reward of being a participant in the writing game.

AVOID
SPUR-OF-THE-MOMENT,
HALF-BAKED IDEAS

This can happen to you (and probably has) if you don't think an idea through before offering it: A top-selling professional unloaded her rage on me as a friend at lunch: "This terrific idea for a hot article popped into my head. I dashed off a note to the magazine. They rejected me. Me . . . with my big reputation! Who the hell do they think they are?"

When I questioned her, she said, "My letter was just three short sentences: 'As you undoubtedly know, I'm an expert on marriage and divorce. How about an article on the shocking rise in teenage divorce? I'll dig up some electrifying facts that will blow the minds of readers.' They sent a rejection slip, not even the courtesy of a personal comment."

I shrugged, "You should be pleased that because of your name they spent the time, effort, and money to send back your note. You indulged in an ego trip, sending a half-baked, spur-of-the-moment flash. You should have thought it through, included a couple of those 'electrifying facts.' "

"Maybe I was hasty. I'll flesh out the facts," she said wryly, "if I can find the time. . . ."

"If *you* won't find the time, you can't expect an editor to put in the time explaining the reason for the rejection."

"HOW CAN I PROTECT
AGAINST HAVING MY IDEAS
STOLEN?"

Yesterday an acquaintance phoned and said, "I've just completed a proposal for a unique exercise book. What do I do now?" I provided some brief tips and suggested he'd find the answers in *Writing Nonfiction that Sells*. He asked the inevitable: "How can I guard against having my great idea stolen?" I sighed, "You can mail a registered or certified copy the same day to yourself—doubtful protection. I've always trusted publishers. I've never been sorry. If they like your 'great idea,' they'll work with you—that's their business."

"Great ideas" don't appear from thin air. For instance: A writer friend who worked in a crowded one-room apartment told me he'd solved interference from his howling baby by releasing the tot to roam; then he'd place himself with typewriter *in the playpen*. I sent the cartoon idea to *The New Yorker* (I've tried almost every kind of writing except porno). Rejected. A few months later, the idea appeared there. I sent a copy of my earlier submission. An editor phoned, said, "The cartoon came in, we liked it, had somehow bypassed your suggestion. We apologize. We didn't steal yours—we constantly receive parallel ideas." I believed him, I know that happens quite often.

I've always conceded that I'm not the only "genius" with totally exclusive concepts. When the cartoon coincidence was explained, I shrugged, "I have lots more ideas in all categories." Again, perhaps I'm too easygoing and trusting. I'm convinced that distrust breeds turndowns.

FIND IDEAS IN YOUR FILES CONTINUALLY

You may be an "organized person," or not. Each of us is different. I *have* to be methodical so that I can use my time most efficiently and effectively for writing. My way is to move ahead step by step. That helps rather than inhibits my creativity, as well as productivity. Here's just one essential, basic way I go about spurring salesworthy ideas: *I find them in my files.*

Going back over a period of more than thirty years, I've been clipping from magazines and newspapers, making notes, filing my findings in category folders. When my subject is "sex," as an example, I go to my file for inspiration and information (items there have been collected for over ten years). To write this particular capsule, I checked my file cabinets (I transformed a sizable dressing closet with a small window into my file room). When I added up, I was astounded to find about a hundred subject files, including these:

Age ... Alcoholism ... Animals ... Anorexia ... Art ... Astrology ... Automobiles ... Brain ... Breathing ... Business ... Cancer ... Children ... Colds ... Communication ... Concentration ... Cooking ... Cosmetics ... Creativity ... Crime ... Customs ... Decorating ... Democracy ... Diet ... Divorce ... Driving ... Drugs ... Education ... Efficiency ... Emotions ... Environment ... Espionage ... Exercise ... Family ... Farming ... Fashion ... Finances ... Foot Health ... Gags and Gimmicks ... Gardening ... Grandparenting ... Happiness ... Headaches ... Health ... Heart ... Herbs ... Holidays ... Homemaking ... House Plants ... Humor ... Ideas, Misc. ... Iguanas ... Interviews ... Love ... Marriage ... Medicine ... Mental Health ... Military ... Money ... Movies ... Music ... Mysteries ... Mysticism ... Nature ... New Book Ideas ... News Gathering ... Nutrition ... Occult ... Optimism ... Parents ... Photography ... Planning ... Politics ... Prejudice ... Productivity ... Psychology ... Publishing ... Racism ... Religion ... Retailing ... Science ... Sex ... Smoking ... Snobbery ... Space ... Sports ... Surgery ... Teens ... Television ... Theater ... Travel ... Twins ... Vacations ... Weather ... Work/Retire ... Writing.

If you keep files, don't necessarily copy or limit yourself to the preceding categories. Like me, you may never get around to using even nearly all the material you've collected. Some of my files contain only a half-dozen items. Others are crowded. No, I don't confine myself to these subjects. I keep eyes and ears, all senses, open for ideas always, without restriction.

Your interests may be entirely different from mine or other writers. Of course! That's all to the good. One secret of enjoying stimulating, rewarding, happy living is *doing what you want to do*. This filing system may spur your own thoughts on idea-finding, along with the other suggestions in this section. You'll decide what will work for you.

Realize, above all, that in creating ideas there is no end: There is only and always the beginning. . . .

SCORE AND SELL WITH THE
S-T-A-R-T SYSTEM

A working method that helped me start selling my writing, instead of having pieces bounce back time after time, is this simple self-checking system:

*S*tudy ideas for your projected piece, focusing on the selling probabilities particularly. What's the market? Check that before you begin.

*T*ake your time picking the subject that interests you most and has the top sales potential. You'll find it far more effective than proceeding on hunch and hope.

*A*rrange your writing procedure in a brief or long outline plan, length depending on the predetermined overall size of the article or book. The estimated number of pages may change as you work along, but it's helpful to have a general guidepost at the start.

*R*echeck S-T-A to be certain you're on the right track in your mind—from start to salable finish.

*T*ype away or start writing in whatever process suits you best. Fill up page after page. Then self-edit repeatedly before you offer the manuscript to the most likely market.

I recommend that you try this S-T-A-R-T System at least several times. Eventually, it will become your natural, personal way to write and sell. Results will prove that it's more beneficial in scoring sales than not planning and monitoring yourself this methodically.

Chapter Five

HOW TO CHOOSE TITLES THAT SELL

Some writers argue, "No use my thinking of an article title. Editors want to create their own titles." That's true—only to a certain extent. I've proved otherwise by topping article submissions with titles—very successfully. Time after time, an editor says, "Your title grabbed me, made me read." (Even if the editorial board changes the title a little or a lot eventually, yours has served its salesmaking purpose.)

It's true that many publications prefer their own titles as being most "compatible" with the magazine philosophy and format. Nevertheless, your first aim with every offering must be to hook the editor's attention firmly—or reading and acceptance may not follow. Results of others, too, support the worth of thinking hard and coming up with a super-grabber title on your submission.

For example, in offering my first gardening article to editors, I didn't say, "Here's helpful gardening advice for your readers." Ho-hum. A beginner, I couldn't take the chance of inducing boredom (one never can!). I dug in, spewed out ideas, offered: "How to Grow a Miracle Garden" (backed with how-tos that worked miracles). Sale!

The candid editor admitted, "Without that title, I'd probably have glanced at your piece, decided that 'we don't need more gardening stuff now.' But I was intrigued—'What's a *miracle* garden?' I realized that our readers would have the same self-serving curiosity to grow not just any old plants, but 'miracles.' "

Even *one* word or a phrase can become the just-right grabber to perform sales miracles, as I touched on earlier. I followed up with other titles to sell a series: "Enjoy a Miracle Rock Garden." "Munch Miracle Herbs from Your Window Sill." "Pick Two-Pound Miracle Tomatoes."

On to a *McCall's* monthly column, "Growing Garden Miracles." Another magazine column: "Miracles for the City Gardener." A King Features Syndicate long-running feature column, "Miracles for Your Garden." A syndicated radio series (wrote and talked hundreds of one-minute segments), "Miracle Gardening Tips." Two top-selling "Miracle" books, *Miracle Gardening*, followed by *Miracle Gardening Encyclopedia*.

The premise and promise behind your title offering must be sound as well as eye-catching. In this case, the foundation was that "a single blade of grass growing from the earth is a miracle," followed through by details of new garden science developments, improved growing methods, materials, devices to produce not just ordinary but "miracle" results. The combination worked for the gardener—and the writer.

Put in the pointed effort to create dramatic, instantly meaningful *title-content combinations* for exceptional successes from your writing efforts.

DIG FOR BURIED TITLES IN YOUR MANUSCRIPT

This unique "digging" tip has worked remarkably for me and others—in mining titles *right from the manuscript* to help make the sale. I came upon this ploy almost by accident. I was urgently seeking a title for an article, aiming for potent words that would grab the editor's attention forcefully. I settled on "How to Get Good Ideas."

As I was writing my covering letter, dissatisfaction nagged at me. I realized that the title was feeble, second-rate. I pushed myself to reread the manuscript once more. *There,* in the second paragraph of the piece about "how to get ideas," the line leaped out at me: ". . . this becomes your key to creative thinking." I changed the title to "Your Key to Creative Thinking." The piece sold. (A great bonus: I used the same title for a very successful book some time later.)

A medical article in *The New Yorker* was titled "The Hoof-beats of a Zebra." I was intrigued, read and enjoyed the fine writing by Berton Roueché. If the article were titled, for instance, "A Case of Myasthenia Gravis" (the subject), I'd never have read it, nor would it attract most editors of popular magazines.

Obviously, the title came from the explanation in the article by a doctor: "There is a saying about diagnoses—about why doctors often fail to recognize one of the less common diseases. It goes, 'When you hear hoofbeats, you don't necessarily think of a zebra.' I recognized the hoofbeats of a zebra."

You'll find that this hunt-and-find ploy is fun, as well as productive in a high percentage of attempts. In one instance, we were visiting a friend when her mail arrived. She grabbed the stack eagerly—then her face fell as she opened a large flat envelope and pulled out a rejected script.

I scanned it, commented, "Your title—'Sex and Marriage'— is flat, no oomph, no hook." Continuing, I stabbed my finger at the middle of the page, read, " 'Greater sexual ecstasy grows from emotional intimacy.' " I suggested, "Build your title around those dynamic words, 'emotional intimacy,' and you'll be halfway to getting the editor involved."

The writer followed through, sold the piece. As it happened, the magazine changed her title for publication. So what? It had worked to focus the needed attention and interest on the worthy manuscript. Try it—this device can work for you, too.

TWO-WAY METHOD TO CREATE YOUR BEST BOOK TITLE

What's in a title or name? Shakespeare wrote that "a rose by any other name would smell as sweet." Not so when you put a name on your book proposal. The title should embody the power to generate intense interest at first sight. Some editors may deny this but, after writing thirty published books, I've been convinced by experience.

How do you pick the *best* name? First . . . while this is not true for every writer, I can't even begin planning or writing a book until I fix a title in my mind and on the page. That's because I look at the title page as the *reader* with eye on the name—either attracted or not right at the starting point. I ask myself and urge that you query yourself: ***Will my proposed title convey and propel the thrust of the book from first line to last?*** The title must help you keep every word right on target. If it doesn't, try for a title that does—and don't stop trying until you get the title that fulfills that test.

Second . . . before I permit myself to feel satisfied about a title, I take a ruled pad and list as many as fifty or more possible names. I may go back to the first finally, but usually I find a more dynamic and precise title along the way. Much more work, but worth it to me. You decide for yourself.

PRETEST YOUR TITLE BY TRYING IT ON OTHERS

This simple pretest can work extraordinarily for you, as it has for me. I always try a title on several people whose judgment I respect exceptionally. A negative reaction doesn't necessarily cause me to eliminate that title, but it sure makes me think again . . . and again. Then I'm more confident if I decide to proceed with that name. Two examples reveal exactly how this process has helped me specifically:

I wasn't happy with my working title for my first diet book with Dr. Irwin M. Stillman. I tried it on a close friend, Oscar Dystel, then head of Bantam Books: "Get That Weight Off Fast!" He reacted, "Awful," . . . then he continued, "What's the point of the book in three words, no more, no less—just three words?"

I thought, said, "It's about *quick weight loss*." He reacted instantly, "That's your title." Later I added "Doctor" to emphasize the M.D. coauthorship: *The Doctor's Quick Weight Loss Diet.* "Quick weight loss" has become part of diet language.

Working on an exposé of Madison Avenue, I told Fredric Dannay, half of the Ellery Queen duo, my working title, *The INSIDE Truth About Advertising.* He frowned, "Not dramatic enough. What's the focus of the book in a few words?" I said, "It's centered on what I call 'permissible lies,' which should not be permissible at all." He approved, "That's your title—*The Permissible Lie.*" That phrase has also become part of the language, often used about politics too.

Significant lesson for you (and me): Both three-word phrases had appeared repeatedly in the body of the manuscripts, but I'd overlooked their potential as titles.

Brief titles are usually most effective, but—as with almost everything in writing and living—sometimes it pays to break the rules. An instance is one of the best-selling titles ever, thirteen words: *Everything You Always Wanted to Know About Sex, but Were Afraid to Ask.*

What's in a title? Could be the difference between success or failure.

SEEK SUBJECTS AND TITLES FROM PAST EXPERIENCE

When you're seeking a subject, a theme, a title for your next writing project, dig into your past life experience. Often you'll come up with valuable material for an article, a series, a book. The following case history shows you how this can work well:

As I've noted, my first diet book, *The Doctor's Quick Weight Loss Diet*, zoomed unexpectedly onto best-seller lists when many individuals lost weight remarkably and told overweight friends, who rushed to buy copies. The publisher phoned excitedly, "We need a follow-up book in a hurry." I said I'd think about it. He urged, "This week, please! Let's not lose the momentum."

First I analyzed fan mail received on the current book, and comments I'd heard from many dieters. They expressed this plea repeatedly: "I've reached my weight-loss goal on the diet, but isn't there some way I can trim my thighs more? They're still bulkier than I'd like." Or the dieter might want to trim upper arms, hips, buttocks, waist, other "problem spots"—the descriptive phrase usually mentioned.

I asked coauthor Dr. Stillman, "Can this trimming be accomplished?"

"Certainly," he stated. "Over the years I've helped many of

my patients trim problem spots with a *low-protein diet.* It pulls fat out of the muscle masses and reduces the areas to the individual's *minimum* personal dimensions. Results are limited, but total size is definitely reduced by inches."

"Is there a way to check?"

"Yes, using a tape measure proves it."

We worked out the right diet, now it needed a name. "Problem spots" has a negative connotation. I wanted something positive. Going back through my files, I found an outstanding ad campaign from my Madison Avenue years. A girdle client needed a name for a new style which featured a concealed band that could be hooked to pull the area tight.

"See," the client said, demonstrating on a model, "the tape measure proves that adjusting the belt more snugly takes inches off the hips and backside." An idea popped—I exclaimed, "Let's name it the *Inches-Off* girdle!" It was an immediate sales success.

Now lightning struck again, based on proved past experience. I came up with "The Doctor's Quick INCHES-OFF Diet." The book became a best-seller as soon as published. Yes, the diet worked as promised, but I doubt whether the book would have sold so many millions of copies without that dramatic, clear-cut "grabber" title.

I recall reading that "the present is the living sum-total of the whole past." Dig into your past experiences, and findings of others, to enhance your writing present and future.

VALUABLE SALESMAKER: THE CLEARLY EXPLANATORY SUBTITLE

Once you settle on an eye-catching title, don't stop there. In many, perhaps most, instances, you need a subtitle to pinpoint and clarify the precise focus and benefit of the book. That works both in your proposal to impress the editor and then in selling to readers when books are in stores.

Note how subtitles add essential salesmaking power to just a few popular books:

- *Eat to Win*
  The Sports Nutrition Bible
- *Up the Organization*
  How to Stop the Corporation from Stifling People and
  Strangling Profits
- *Conscious Happiness*
  How to Get the Most out of Living
- *In Search of Excellence*
  Lessons from America's Best Run Companies
- *"Doctor, Make Me Beautiful!"*
  A Leading Plastic Surgeon Tells You Everything
  You Want to Know About Cosmetic Surgery

Without the explanatory subtitles in these and many other successful nonfiction books and articles, prospective purchasers might easily miss understanding the full potential benefits provided in the volume. Sales executives in any business will affirm that puzzlement blocks buying. Put the power of subtitles to work for you in your articles as well as books.

Chapter Six

DEVELOP WORK METHODS TO HELP YOU SELL

At a large party, a boor interrupted a conversation among several writers, "Big deal—it's a cinch to write, anybody can do it!"

"Sure," I agreed, "you just put your hands on the typewriter keys . . . and let your fingers go."

Does that way work to produce writing that sells? Perhaps for a far-out genius. I tried it and it didn't bring forth a single word or earn a penny for me. I had to develop the work methods that work for me always, now passed along to you.

ORGANIZE . . . TO WRITE NONFICTION THAT SELLS

Starting Something New? Start a File

Whether it's a short piece, a longer article, or a book, I find it *absolutely essential* to start a file for the project—to "arrange in a systematic manner." That method keeps the ideas and information flowing smoothly for the benefit of the reader (and for me). The system saves you time and energy. And, very important, it *reduces stress*.

Once you're organized, you eliminate much confusion and

many foul-ups. You proceed with preplanned progression. You're not in a turmoil, slowed up by hunting around for items you've put "somewhere" but don't know exactly where. I recommend strongly that you get into the organizing habit. You'll thank me forevermore.

Here, precisely, is the methodology I've evolved: I use a fire-retardant file cabinet (for peace of mind, replacing fear about work in progress going up in flames). The sturdy metal file I use is a relatively small size, 9½" wide by 14" long by 11" deep. Takes regular hanging file folders. Actually, I use three such file cabinets: one for articles in progress, another for the current book I'm writing, and a third for the next book I'm planning.

Of course, you can use any kind of file you want, an ordinary low-cost file box, even a grocery carton. The most important factor is that you have your material at your fingertips in some kind of orderly sequence—always subject to shifting and change as you work along.

Here's how I forge ahead from start to finish: First I outline the structure of the article or book, separating the subject matter into segments (chapters, for a book). I label a hanging file folder for each segment. As I work along, jotting ideas, notes, details, I drop each sheet in turn into the allocated file folder.

Then, when I'm ready to write the total article or book, I reach into the contents of each folder in progression. I proceed step by step until the end, the pages piling up in sequence. When that's done, I work along with my reviewing, adding, rewriting—through to the satisfactory completed manuscript.

If the piece I'm writing is quite short and uncomplicated, a few ordinary file folders kept together, one upon the other on a corner of my desk, may be sufficient. To help keep my mind clear, avoiding confusion, I have handy file folders in various colors, a different color for each article. You'll work out for yourself the little tricks and routines that you find are most helpful personally.

Your working procedure is your own choice, naturally. I'm not dictating any hard-and-fast rules that must be followed. I created my orderly systems because writing to a quality standard that sells is tough enough without imposing on myself the extra burden of being disorganized. That would block me badly, as I strive to set down one clear, communicative sentence after another.

When I've shown visiting writers my work-in-progress file system, I've often had the reaction, "I wish I was that organized, then maybe I could produce as much as you do." I explain that I'm "so organized" because I couldn't possibly be a productive, *earning* author otherwise. Try it. See what an enormous difference it makes in the quality and profitability of what you write.

Organizing an Article That Sells

Here's how I organized an article that I sold to *Ladies' Home Journal*, one of the first I offered after I moved into my career as a full-time free-lance writer. The proposal the editor bought was for a short piece on a women's movement which started in Kansas City, Missouri. As I organized the available information, the piece grew into a lengthy cover story titled, "How Mothers Fight Prejudice: Panel of American Women."

Another vital point for you to absorb and profit from: If I hadn't set up a systematized file and followed through by gathering, classifying, and categorizing the considerable factual material, the idea probably wouldn't have developed and grown into a major lead article earning top payment. This is a detailed example of what *you* can do to increase your writing sales and fees:

Recognize the possibility: At a large dinner party, a visitor from the West mentioned that she was a participant in a new women's movement to fight prejudice. That struck me as having article potential. After dinner I talked at length with the visiting guest. I obtained details about the group called Panel of American Women. I turned that into a magazine proposal which clicked. Two other writers present overlooked the opportunity.

Organize the material: From what I'd learned thus far, I set up a systematized series of files labeled:

A. Purpose of the Panel of American Women
B. How the panel began
C. A typical panel program
D. How panel members are selected
E. Profiles of four panel members

F. Short talks given by panel members

G. Audience reactions and responses

H. Actual results in fighting prejudice

I. How to start a panel in your community

J. Dramatic future promise for local panels and
individual panel members.

Mail response to the article was extraordinary, delighting
the magazine. Panels sprang up in many communities. Editors of
other publications, too, noticed the feature and asked me to write
for them.

There are two prime lessons for you here, in addition to the
resultful step-by-step way to organize and sell your writing:

1. Recognize and cash in on opportunities for stories that embody something original and angles often not readily appar-
ent to others.

2. Don't be thwarted by any lack of past successful experience.
Realize—worth repeating—that this was one of the first
nonfiction pieces I worked on as a full-time free-lance writer. You, too, can score, just as I did with this early article
and enterprising writing thereafter.

Organizing a Book That Sells

Here, as a precise model to consider for your own potential writing achievements, is the promising outline I organized to help
create my first nonfiction book.

I'd written two published mystery novels which were actually pretty wild burlesques of the Madison Avenue advertising
world. (As a beleaguered adman, this writing helped me let off
steam, reducing some of the frantic pressure.) Part of my work
was writing garden advertising, necessitating digging up much
valuable information. Also, I'd been an able, enthusiastic gardener since childhood.

The masterful head of Bantam Books, Oscar Dystel, noting
my garden products advertising, requested a presentation for an
original Bantam paperback. Intrigued, I drew on my advertising
agency experience. I organized a chapter outline for a proposed

book, as if planning a million-dollar campaign for approval by a prospective advertising client. Here's my segmented structure:

I listed the most important subjects to interest and inform home gardeners. I filled a file box with hanging folders for twenty-two chapters. Then I inserted material in each applicable folder from extensive research and notes. Result—this organized structure:

1. How to GROW a MIRACLE GARDEN
2. "Miracle Pointers" for BEAUTIFUL LAWNS
3. Using FERTILIZERS for Miracle Results
4. Benefits from SOIL CONDITIONERS and GROWTH BOOSTERS
5. Applying INSECTICIDES and FUNGICIDES Effectively
6. Musts for PREPARING SOIL, PLANTING, MULCHING
7. Up-to-Date PROPAGATION Miracles
8. Growing ANNUALS for Glorious Color
9. Planting PERENNIALS for Enduring Beauty
10. ROSES for Special Garden Radiance
11. Exciting BULBS, CORMS, TUBERS
12. Enjoy Delicious, Nutritious SUPER-VEGETABLES
13. Pick Bigger and Better BERRIES
14. Select Scintillating SHRUBS, TREES, VINES
15. Special Tips for Superior HOUSE PLANTS
16. Delight in Multicolored AFRICAN VIOLETS
17. Multiply Your Pleasure with HERB PLANTINGS
18. Bonus Rewards: ROCK GARDENS and GROUND COVERS
19. Explore New Worlds in a GREENHOUSE
20. Get Longer-Lasting Beauty from CUT FLOWERS
21. More Power from POWER and Other EQUIPMENT
22. YOU—the Greatest Garden Miracle of All!

This comprehensive listing, springing from thorough organization of gardeners' needs, brought swift approval from the editorial director. A shallow, slipshod proposal would have died.

Based on solid planning, the manuscript developed swiftly and smoothly. Combining clear, factual instruction with joy and inspiration, the book went through many editions, spawned four more gardening books.

Proof: It pays to organize your writing for in-depth success.

How to G-R-O-W a Book

Usually, the biggest barrier blocking writers, especially a beginner, from tackling a nonfiction book is becoming terrified due to staring up at that huge mountain of words you have to climb. Even if you have no intention of ever tackling a book, this can be a valuable lesson for your future as a writer. Organizing properly, as described, clarifies and simplifies the task. It works when you proceed step by step this way:

When I first started writing creatively, an article of a thousand words loomed as an intimidating challenge, almost an insurmountable one. After I managed that a few times, a five-thousand-word piece seemed a little less difficult, but still practically impossible.

From there, your courage and confidence keep growing. Make yourself keep moving on another mile, another thousand words at a time, to twenty-thousand-word articles. Don't stop there! Move ahead, screwing up your stamina, spilling the well-known blood, sweat, and tears, to a sixty-thousand-word book. Then it becomes a bit easier, but you have to keep pushing.

When I finally finished a rather mammoth, instructive gardening encyclopedia of more than a hundred thousand words, I found that I had passed a milestone—as you can discover eventually. You'll realize that—while it's still difficult, and never *really* easy—you have lots more confidence and less hesitation than when writing the first thousand-word piece.

Book Building:
One-Page-at-a-Time System

This simple but priceless pointer can lead you to profitable new areas: The most helpful step, I've found, in building a book—after organizing a chapter-by-chapter framework—is: ***Get moving, set*** *down your first page*—on a pad with pen or pencil, or with typewriter or word processor, whatever way is most comfortable for you. Extremely important: ***Don't even think about the last page!***

This One-Page-at-a-Time System can work for you, as it has for me—through thirty books now and an infinite (well, almost) number to go. I still use this system in starting every new book. Above all, never look toward your final objective and worry, "It's so far away!" Instead, concentrate on the first page, then onward, each page at a time, not concerning yourself about the end.

When I finish the first page, I tell myself happily, "Great— I've made a start—I have a page down in writing" (even though I may rewrite it a dozen times eventually). Then I move ahead, focusing only on the first fifty pages of a three-hundred-page manuscript. When I finish page 50, I cheer, "One-sixth of the pages done already"—not moaning, "Still five-sixths of the way to go."

At page 101, I tell myself eagerly, "Over one-third finished." At page 151, triumphantly, "I'm past the halfway mark, the top of the mountain—all downhill now, comparatively easy going." It makes all the difference in self-motivation and productive impetus when you accent the positive, thus eliminating the negative. This "half-full" rather than "half-empty" attitude enables you to appreciate the amount of ground you've covered, rather than the distance you still have to go. You'll find that making a start, then moving ahead one step at a time energetically, will be a major development in writing and selling longer and longer pieces.

As you stretch your writing muscles, finally you have a book in hand. That will be infinitely rewarding for you, as you make the ecstatic discovery that, unlike an article, a book is *forever*. I'm thrilled in advance for you.

E-X-P-A-N-D Articles into Books

As you write articles and sell them—which you will, even if you haven't scored up to this point—*be sure to save all your background and research material on each piece*. There are two primary rewards at hand:

1. Use the data to help write and sell more articles on the same subject or similar themes.

2. With enough articles on the overall topic, consider expanding them into a book.

Case history: Exemplifying the first point . . . As I was working in advertising, involved in all its phases, I started writing articles for the advertising and business trade publications. I sold one piece, then others on different facets of advertising and marketing. Dozens of such informative pieces appeared, including: "Creating the Big Selling Ideas" . . . "How to Re-Energize Old Products" . . . "Getting Top Results from Research" . . . and on and on.

This sparked the second reward: An alert editor at Doubleday & Company (who later moved on to notable national government positions) saw and read the articles. He tracked me down and suggested that I submit an outline for a book. That led to one of my earliest published books, *Successful Ideas for Advertising and Selling*.

The files I'd kept, loaded with material which I'd used as resource data for the pieces, provided a treasure to mine when I began writing the book. I added new material, and the manuscript chapters grew readily, covering "Creating Big Selling Ideas," "Re-Energizing Old Products," "Top Research Results"— fourteen chapters in all. This successful book was one of the easiest to write, thanks to the articles from which it had sprouted. (I've used here some basic material from my pieces in various publications.)

Consider added sales opportunities by studying your articles, books, and other writing again and again for spin-offs that can be developed and sold to the same or other publishers. Two examples:

1. In a published article on losing weight, I noted I'd mentioned that a small percentage of overly thin individuals seek to *gain* weight. I queried the editor on that point, resulting in the sale to him of a piece on how to put on pounds.

2. My book, *Your Key to Creative Thinking*, included a number of "mental-exercise puzzlers," challenging and intriguing quickie posers. These attracted so much favorable fan mail

that I alerted *Reader's Digest,* which bought and printed some in several worldwide issues. I probably could have collected many more puzzlers and approached book publishers if I'd wished.

You'll often find such buried treasure in your own writing, but only if you dig for it.

Sprout Articles and Other Earnings from Books

It's vital for you to realize, in considering writing a book eventually, if not now, to regard a book as the *beginning* of exceptional earning power. It's up to *you* to make a book sprout added income for yourself from every possible source.

Here's a specific demonstration of how you can multiply other bounty from a book: You noted earlier how my *Miracle Gardening* original paperback grew from my gardening advertising work. That volume was just the start, as I used it as a springboard for proliferating gardening "crops" in many areas, as follows . . .

1. I expanded the *Miracle Gardening* book into a follow-up massive hardcover, *Miracle Gardening Encyclopedia.* Instead of stopping there, three further books were developed:

    Samm Baker's Clear & Simple Gardening Handbook provided breezy, intimate all-over information for gardeners, in hardcover and paperback editions. A very popular book followed, whose purpose was to bring children of all ages into the wonderful world of gardening, via fun and games—*The Indoor & Outdoor GROW-IT Book.* A different, intriguing slant developed into *Gardening Do's and Don'ts.* That made a total of five books before I moved to other fields.

2. Many magazine articles stemmed from subjects in the books—rock gardens, growing better house plants, longest life for cut flowers, lots more. Note that you'd never have to run out of prospects to write and earn from just one popular topic.

3. A continuing column, which combined a number of brief tips in each issue, ran month after month in *McCall's*.

4. A King Features syndicated series appeared in many newspapers nationwide during the prime growing seasons year after year.

5. A syndicated radio series was created, in which I wrote and vocally delivered hundreds of fifty-second gardening tips (preceded by five-second identifications by individual local sponsors at beginning and end of the tip, followed by a one-minute commercial by the sponsor). The series continued in markets all over the country for many years.

All these bonus earnings developed from just one book as a result of a writer discerning and appraising the potentials, then working to maximize them aggressively. **You can do the same.**

Write for Top Quality: "Up," Never "Down"

You must write to your highest personal standard unfailingly—to *communicate clearly* with your reader. The more you try to write your best, the better you must become. Only if you let down on *yourself* will you let down the reader.

Ignore inflated, self-loving individuals who demean any writing that is not their own. By calling nonfiction "trash" or "nonbooks," they seek to show that they are "better than" others. Pity and flee such "better than" people; they don't realize how empty and contemptible they are.

Be proud of writing *your* way, for the best possible result you can achieve. I've run into puffheads who try to boost their egos by belittling me, for example, as a "nonfiction" or "self-help" or "how-to" author. A friend once asked, "Doesn't that make you feel inferior about your writing?" I smiled, "Nobody can make me feel inferior about my writing or anything else—*without my permission.*"

I recommend that attitude to you for your writing and everything in living. All the ways-that-work in these pages are provided to help you build and raise your writing standard, ability, and earning power. Aim and work toward your best—then *you can't miss.*

Challenge Yourself: "Have I Earned the Right to Sell?"

Study this case for clarifying self-analysis about your potentially profitable writing career: Bruno, a smart, tough, outspoken man who owned one of the top-rated gourmet resaurants in America, told me, "I was very poor, worked in meat slaughtering, learned about food. Fought my way up in the restaurant world. I just gave my first article about my experiences to a big magazine editor-in-chief who eats free in my place. Watch for my writing, I'm going to be *big*."

A week later, he phoned angrily, came over to our house, thrust a manuscript at me. "That damned fool editor turned this down," he raged. "It's a masterpiece! What the hell does he know about the writing business? Read it."

I read. "Exciting, bloody stuff here," I said quietly. "But it charges erratically all over the place. It's incoherent. You must learn to write by writing, rewriting, again and again. You have dramatic things to say—you'll make it."

As he was about to explode at me, I raised my hand as a stop sign. "I've advised you," I said. "Now I want some expert advice from you in return." A generous man, he nodded. "I plan to open a fine restaurant with two other writers in a location two blocks from you. We're sure it'll be an instant success—"

He roared, "You're crazy—you'll lose your shirt! What the hell do you know about the restaurant business?"

I echoed quietly, "Bruno, what the hell do you know about the writing business?"

He glowered, grabbed his manuscript, spat, "The hell with writing, I haven't the time to learn. . . ."

How about you? You keep learning as you keep writing. If you do, you'll make it. The Brunos of the world never will. They haven't *earned* the right to be published.

Pinpoint Your Special Place for Highest Productivity

Joan, a prolific writer, told me, "Until I found my 'special place,' I had trouble getting started each day. I yearned to be tucked away somewhere. I thought about it, located my 'secret spot' in a tiny attic room. Now, even as I climb the creaking stairs, ideas start popping." She laughed. "If I'm tempted to answer the phone or doorbell, I think of hauling my butt up those steep steps again. So I stay put, not interrupting my writing flow." She has a big, beautiful home, but chooses that remote cell. Well, nobody ever accused us writers of being "normal."

I've met authors who say they do their best work on their feet, filling a pad propped on a high music stand. When I commuted for years between home and Madison Avenue, I concocted ideas and articles on the train (I'm writing this now in a railway car headed for a publisher meeting—"conditioned reflex"). I've read that "Thomas Wolfe managed to write almost endlessly using a lead pencil on grocery bags spread on top of the icebox."

Jerry (you've read his stuff) sweated out his early ideas and writing on a small desk in the busy, crowded living room, wife and kids running by, vacuum cleaner buzzing. He complained constantly about noise and interruptions. He scored, built a studio annex all his own. He just couldn't write there. Stalled for a couple of months, he's back in the congested, noisy living room, happily griping—and writing.

How about you? It may help you to list what might be your best places for creative thinking and writing—indoors and outdoors. Perhaps one spot will lift your productivity automatically without preventing your writing elsewhere. You may even find that you concentrate best on a bus, but don't miss your stop!

Train Yourself to Be an
Everywhere Writer

Let's not delude ourselves—we writers are not all the same. We can't all write similarly or work identically. We don't want to. Expressing your individuality is one of the great boons of succeeding in the wonderful world of writing. If you think that a writer must work in an ivory tower, these revealing facts—proving how some earning writers adapt to circumstances—can be very helpful.

You have a choice of ivory tower or the power of *concentration*. Motivate yourself to concentrate on your project, and you can write anywhere. Holding a full-time advertising job, I had to snatch time to write on my own. So I wrote most of my articles and first nine books on commuting trains to and from New York City offices.

Care enough to concentrate wherever you are. . . or wonder whether you are a truly dedicated writer. I carried manuscripts with me always, and still do when traveling. As a beginner, I'd write on a bus, in reception rooms, in the living room with our kids doing their homework and Natalie sketching in an armchair so we could all be together. Nothing special about me, but I knew that if I wanted to be an earning writer, *I had to write no matter what or where.*

In an interview for a magazine personality series (I conducted research and interviews out of office hours), author Betty Smith told me that she wrote her best-selling *A Tree Grows in Brooklyn* "on the kitchen table while cooking for my two growing daughters. Divorced, I supported them by writing a mass of one-act plays and articles, then *Tree*, because I *had* to do it that way."

Famed artist Dong Kingman, coauthor of articles and books with his writer wife, Helena, always carries a sketch pad like an extension of his hand, as Helena writes in her notebook on the current assignment. Wherever Dong is, at a play, on a plane, in a restaurant, he draws sketches which turn into fast-selling watercolors—just as you can do, expanding your jotted notes into articles and books.

There are innumerable similar examples proving that eight simple words can guide you to writing success: *To write, you gotta write wherever you are!* Concentrate and publish.

Choose the Writing Process
That Suits You

Don't make the mistake of wasting time agonizing about what writing method is best, especially under pressure from wild-eyed word processor enthusiasts. How you write depends on "What's best for me?" Too many individuals use the self-imposed dilemma as an excuse for delaying and not writing words they can sell.

One insists "pen and ink" . . . another, "manual typewriter" . . . "correcting electric" . . . "word processor or you're in the Dark Ages." They're right about themselves. And all wrong for others. Author Muriel Spark rejected word processing: "I still write with a pen, in a notebook. Each notebook has seventy-two pages. I write on every other line, on one side of the page. It adds up." That's the crux: *"It adds up."* You can sell effective words scrawled first on a brown supermarket bag. Do it your way, as long as it adds up.

Word processors can perform miracles of timesaving efficiency in correcting, editing, shuffling words, lines, paragraphs, pages. I'm all for them for those who can work best that way. **But a word processor cannot write for you creatively, individually, personally** . . . after all, it's only *inhuman.* Enjoy *your* intimate way to write and sell. In the final analysis, the *quality* of the writing makes the sale—or misses the boat.

"Can I Hold a Job and Write After Hours?" Sure You Can!

Would-be writers ask me the foregoing question repeatedly . . . and skeptically. If it applies to you, ask yourself instead, "Do I want *enough* to be a selling writer?" Do you? *The proof is in writing enough*—wherever and whenever there's a possible moment available.

I assure you, from solid evidence, that you *can* hold a full-time or part-time job—even run a household—and still *write and sell.* I've met countless individuals, successful selling writers, who've done just that. Examples:

A best-selling writer, a homemaker, who raised two daughters after a divorce, without support money, wrote her head off at the kitchen table every minute she could snatch . . . writing, writing . . . then a sale here, a sale there . . . finally a blockbuster. Work full-time? part-time? She worked *double*-time—and finally scored!

A recent college graduate confronted me: "I want to be a writer and work in publishing, but no jobs are open." On questioning, I learned that, like most hopefuls, he'd sought only *editorial* work. I advised, "Try for *any* job, no matter how menial or low paying." He finally started at a publishing company as a messenger boy: He was *in.* He wrote after hours, weekends, began selling free-lance. He kept writing, and advancing in business. He's now a beleaguered advertising executive who still *keeps writing,* has had many articles and three books published.

An ambitious newspaper reporter complained, "I write so much at work all day, I can't write my own stuff at night because I'm written out, need a change." I told her that I'd made a thrilling discovery years earlier: After writing ads all day in the office, I found relief writing *my own stuff my way for me,* nights and weekends. She phoned me months later: "It works. Writing for the job by day, then for me at night, they're totally different. I just sold a magazine article that I wouldn't have tackled before."

Ask yourself again now, please: "Do I care enough to become a selling writer . . . to work at something else and write, too?" It's tough, but I *know* that you can. You'll prove it only by writing in every "spare" hour and even minute you can find.

Important P.S.: If you have a job now and need the income, my imperative advice is that when you start selling what you write, *don't give up your job right away.* One or a few sales don't guarantee a career, and you may find yourself in financial trouble. When you're earning enough and are sufficiently confident of a steady income from writing, then you might consider leaving your job for full-time writing.

Of course, you'll do what you personally decide. I simply urge you to *think twice*—lest you stop too soon and then fall off a fiscal precipice if your money runs out. Whatever decision you make, I wish you success and happiness.

How to Break Through "Writer's Block"

A desperate professional author, Hank, asked at a Writers' Lunch Seminar, "How can I break through my hopeless writer's block? It throws me every now and then, more often lately. It drives me crazy, especially now halfway through my new book. It's terrible. I sit and stare at the blank page on my typewriter, can't find words or ideas, can't get going. *Help!*"

I told him my method: "No matter how reluctant and empty-headed I feel, I roll an empty sheet into my typewriter, put my fingers on the keys. **Then I force myself to hammer out words and sentences.** No matter what I write, even utter gibberish, I keep slogging. By the bottom of the page, I'm started, I'm moving, making sense. . . .

"I keep filling up pages. Soon I see real headway. I stop and reread from the start, keeping the next sheet ready in the typewriter. I correct, rewrite—or start over. I find, and I think you'll discover, Hank, that by using this gobbledygook attack, *you're writing . . . you keep writing . . .* and you come up with a clear, salable manuscript."

Hank phoned excitedly the next morning. "Your attack-keep-going method worked. I hit the keys, words started to flow, the dam burst. I'm turning out good stuff!"

It's easy to give in to "writer's block" if you don't fight it through nonstoppable action, as described. I don't know whether that frustrating blockage is a genuine, honest psychological phenomenon, or laziness, or a general human inclination to goof off, go fishing, or just lie in the sun. Whatever it is, I've overcome any such inclination by *Doing*, not giving in, not stopping dead. If you knuckle under to writer's block, you're not writing—and, if so, are you a writer?

Some top-selling authors on "writer's block." Best-selling author Gore Vidal, in a *Publishers Weekly* interview, commented brutally: "When I hear about writer's block, this one and that one! f*** off! Stop writing, for Christ's sake, you're not meant to be doing this. Plenty more where you came from."

In a different *PW* interview, the extraordinary Isaac Bashevis Singer told what he does: *"I work!* I don't go in for fancy excuses. I never moan and groan that I'm blocked. So some days it doesn't come [a shrug]. But you write anyway and fix it the next day. You work and you labor because you want to see the results. It feels good to go into stores and see your book."

A beginner asked juvenile science writer Vicki Cobb, as she signed books in a store, "Do you ever get writer's cramp?" She said, "Yes . . . but it's not anything as bad as writer's block."

Popular author Marlene Shyer stated bluntly, "I hate writing. But I hate *not writing* even more!"

Perhaps the simplest solution is *to love writing*.

Solution to Frustration About Writing: "I DO MY WORK!"

This tip has helped me immeasurably—I pass it on to you for the first time anywhere: Our wise and famous artist friend Dong

Kingman was walking with me near the sea. We spoke of the frustrations of being an artist and a writer—interruptions, demands by others (perhaps in your case having a household or a pressure job), lack of understanding, rejections. . . .

I asked, "Dong, how do you handle the barrage of outside problems and blockages?"

He stopped in midstep, said flatly: *"I do my work! I keep painting. I DO MY WORK!"*

Next time you feel it's all just too much to handle, that you can't go on writing, set your butt firmly on the chair, say out loud, **"I do my work!"** Begin to hammer away until the words start to flow . . . and away you go. . . .

Plan Future Articles
and Books NOW

You may not be ready to write on a particular salable subject now, but you should be collecting material, even years ahead. Here's how you'll turn subjects into sales—in four successive steps that get you there:

1. List subjects of high reader interest for short pieces, comprehensive articles, syndicated features, books. As an example, my files have included: How Advertising Works and Doesn't Work . . . Selling Ideas That Build Sales . . . How-To Gardening . . . Keys to Creative Thinking . . . Diets for Slimming and Good Health . . . Fitness Programs for Men and Women . . . Getting the Most out of Life . . . Better Sex for Everyone . . . on and on.

2. Open a file on each subject. Week after week, make copies or cut out items pertinent to the subject from magazines, newspapers, books. Take notes of information heard on radio and TV, in conversations, anywhere. Place the clips and notes in the applicable files.

3. Keep thinking of subjects in the back of your mind. As you get useful thoughts and ideas, write them down. Slip the notes in the proper files.

4. When ready to write on a subject, dig into the file. You'll find a treasury of material for a selling piece or book. My diet file, for instance, filled over a ten-year period, proved invaluable in utilizing many of the assorted bits in writing published articles and best-selling books. I researched and filed material on "sex" for more than twelve years before writing a book on that highly marketable subject.

Pick *your* subjects. These four basic steps will put you way ahead in writing and finishing salable manuscripts when you're ready to go-go-go.

Don't "Talk About" Writing . . . Write It!

The following happens to me repeatedly, a smiling lady telling me, "I'm going to write a book someday. How do I go about it?" I ask, "Let's see what you've written." Surprised. "Oh, I haven't written yet. I'm *going* to write a book." I tell her and you: "Talking about writing isn't writing. Put words down actually, or you're nothing, nowhere."

Another of many such letters arrived yesterday: "I read a magazine article about your writing career. I want to write an article about changes in our family's life-style due to economic conditions. . . ." I replied, " 'Wanting to' is a waste. *Start writing!*"

Any day you're reluctant to start writing, which happens to most individuals occasionally, reread the S-T-A-R-T System and other ways-that-work in these pages. Then do what I and other professionals do: Set your butt solidly and start and *keep writing*. Beyond anything else, a writer is one who writes, who produces words. Anything else signifies little or nothing.

Right now, stop reading . . . *get going, get words down visibly . . . and keep going!*

Finish What You Start

If you're well into a writing project, turning out one or more satisfying pages, then find it very tough going, I urge you to *keep pushing*, keep writing. Then reread and reedit after every few pages. If, after trying repeatedly, you still consider it hopeless, that's time enough to discard.

Chances are, however, that by the time you've made sizable headway, you'll be motivated to restudy, revise, edit exhaustively. Happily, you'll then have a solid selling piece—especially now that you're writing toward a sound marketing goal every time.

On the other hand, if you quit before you're well into the piece, or have finished it, that would be as though you stopped dead after ninety-nine yards of a hundred-yard dash. There's no way you could win that race—in running or writing.

In my experience, if you've planned well according to the S-T-A-R-T System, it pays to push to the finish. I started a diet book that I believed in thoroughly. My presentation included a detailed chapter outline and two complete chapters, usually more than enough. The presentation was rejected by one publisher after another because, as each stated (true then), "Diet books aren't selling."

"If at first you don't succeed . . ." I kept on doggedly, piling up manuscript pages through a storm of turndowns for more than a year, despite the fact that some writers and agents consider this course "unprofessional." I ignored the hidebound "professional" shibboleths, as you may do anytime you wish. I believed almost fanatically in this book's exceptional merit and best-seller potential, so was too stupid to be stopped.

At last I finished the manuscript, realizing that the time and effort expended could be a total loss. My steadfast agent kept the faith, trying one publisher after another. We hoped that the marketing attitude would change, but it didn't. Finally, two years after I met my doctor-coauthor, the seventeenth editor approached told her bosses forcefully that this book was "going to be a block-buster." She insisted that it be accepted or else she would resign because it would mean that they didn't have enough regard for her judgment.

Fortunately for me, she had a lot of power because she worked with some top authors who would have followed her to a new affiliation. Even though the editorial board turned thumbs down on the manuscript, the beleaguered publisher put it out, but with little advertising or publicity. Sales started climbing, nevertheless, as one dieter after another lost pounds and inches, and told others who told others who told others . . . .

That volume, *The Doctor's Quick Weight Loss Diet*, became the #2 best-selling diet book of all time. I shudder (and so does Natalie) to even think about the loss if I had abandoned it early on. There's a moral: ***If YOU don't believe enough in your writing, who will?***

Finish One, Start Another Project

The day-after-day writing system—***Finish One, Start Another Project***—is part of the regular, orderly, systematic writing procedure that works for many other successful writers, as well as for me. It can work for you to attain a steady, sizable writing income if you will work with it.

There's no mystery, no secret here, but you have to *do it*—not put off until tomorrow what you can write today. Very simply: When you finish one piece of writing, whether it's a short document, a longer article, or a book, you then start almost immediately on the next project. You don't necessarily begin writing the new work in the next minute. You do proceed with your organizing, research, and then go on to setting down one page after another.

John Creasey, the noted author who wrote some nonfiction but primarily mystery and suspense novels, probably turned out more mystery books, under more than a dozen pseudonyms, than any other writer ever. He described his particular system to me as working for him with nonfiction or fiction: As soon as he finished the manuscript of a book, he'd send it off to two critics he employed. They would write their reactions, comments, and suggestions about the manuscript and shoot it back.

Creasey explained that he barely put down the last page of a manuscript before he started the next. When he finished that one, he'd send it on to his two readers, then tackle the previous one which they had criticized. He'd work that over thoroughly, have it retyped, funneled to a publisher. In that way, he said, he always had some piece of writing being read by editors, producing for him, resulting in a steady stream of sales. That was *his* way. I pretty much work similarly, except that I'm my own critic. (Natalie helps me greatly by going over my drafts, as someone close may be able to do for you.)

No, I'm not trying to strap you into a straitjacket of conformity. You'll work *your* way, since you, like every other writer, are an individual, proceeding in your individual fashion. That's one of the prime blessings of being a writer, *you do it your way*. If you haven't discovered it already, you'll find your own best working strategy as you proceed from one manuscript to another.

I pass on to you the effective Finish-Start system of writing as one method that helps me and others write to sell and accomplishes that successfully. If you try this process, you'll accomplish most by keeping after it from one manuscript to the next *repeatedly*. Your successes are bound to develop and grow.

Develop and Practice Patience to Endure as a Writer

"At the least, bear patiently, if thou canst not joyfully," wrote author Thomas à Kempis over five hundred years ago. His advice becomes increasingly valuable, since you face mounting modern frustration as you await:

- *Replies to your publication submissions:* Often months.
- *Response to book proposals and presentations:* Up to six months or more for single submissions and up to three months or more for multiple submissions, unless you specify "reply within thirty days, please," which may bring no answer at all.
- *Waiting for magazine publication* after acceptance: Up to a year or more.
- *Delay in book publication* after manuscript delivered: Usually about a year, sometimes more.

There are exceptions, but such grueling delays can make you climb the walls if you don't know the facts of publishing life and don't master patience. Are the lengthy waits justified or necessary? Publishers state with some validity that they are understaffed, to avoid heavy overhead and losses. Business organization is so complicated and ponderous, especially in the giant houses and conglomerates, that routines grind along sluggishly step by step.

Delays *justified?* Perhaps. *Essential?* Absolutely not! A "hot" article can appear in a weekly within a week, in a monthly within two months or less. Complex paperback "specials" ("instant books") such as the *Report of the Warren Commission* are on the racks within a week or so from start to finish. *The Complete Scarsdale Medical Diet* was shipped in hardcover about two months after we delivered the final manuscript. It's difficult, but it can be done when somebody up there orders: *"Do it!"*

Solution for the writer: I've learned through necessity to manage justified feelings of impatience and frustration this way: As soon as I finish a short or long manuscript and send it off, I don't wait anxiously and suffer. Instead, *I start on a new writing project immediately.* I always have other undertakings in the planning and research stages. As I complete this book, I have extensive file material and notes on three articles and three books to submit, prepare proposals and presentations, and write. While awaiting responses, I'm actually already writing the article or book I've selected as my first priority. Yes: finish/start.

Certainly I get some recurrent pangs of irritation and indignation about the delays. I don't groan and give up. I keep pressing editors for a resolution pleasantly, positively, constructively. It's destructive to get anyone mad at me. Editors usually have even more severe frustrations and anxieties, due to entanglements and obstructions in an organizational setup—pressure from others that we lucky writers who operate alone don't encounter every working hour.

So I keep going, *I do my work.* You're an individual and may not be able to manage your temperament this way, but it's worth trying. It works for me and many others (not all) whom I've advised through the years.

Chapter Seven

DEVELOP A STYLE THAT SELLS

"The style of an author should be the image of his [or her] mind, but the choice and command of language is the fruit of exercise." Edward Gibbon wrote that over two hundred years ago; the essence is just as valid today. The ways-that-work which follow will help you develop a solid, personal style that pays off. Artificial attempts and quirky shortcuts invariably will fail you in writing to sell.

Style evolves from being yourself, writing your personal truth, not trying to imitate or to be anyone else, not attempting to write "fancy" or artificially highbrow. Don't try to develop a writing style self-consciously; let it emerge naturally from the inside out. For example. . . .

A man in one of my classes showed me an article he had written about race riots. It had been turned down by several magazines. He explained, puzzled, "I happened to be an observer at a race riot which flared up suddenly. I saw an innocent passerby, like myself, knocked over and almost trampled to death before police rescued her. I figured that would make an exciting piece, but editors don't seem to think so."

He sat alongside me as I read the article, watched as I shook my head negatively, "It doesn't grab me."

He objected, "What's wrong? I tried to plaster on lots of excitement. Don't you find a race riot stirring?"

"Not the way you wrote it," I said. "The situation certainly promises excitement and stimulation, but your article didn't bring it out. You didn't involve me as a reader, didn't make me feel I was there in person. You could have pulled me right into the middle of the action, the confusion, the terror. . . ."

I suggested, as I recommend to you repeatedly, "Restudy the article as the reader, not as the writer."

He returned later. "You're right—I saw my mistakes clearly when I reread what I'd written. I'd put down what occurred *from the outside looking in,* rather than taking the reader right into the middle of the mess where I had been."

I advised further, "You'll have a better chance to make a sale if you extend the article beyond the personal experience angle. Do some research. Add interviews with experts. Help the reader not only experience a race riot but also understand the larger problems."

Months later, he phoned and said that he'd followed through. "Just received an acceptance from a Sunday newspaper magazine. Took a lot more time and effort, but it was worth it."

REEXAMINE: DON'T TELL "ABOUT" WHAT HAPPENED

Recheck your writing to be sure you don't make this common error: In a writing seminar, students wrote something at home, read it in class, then others commented on it. In about 85 percent of cases, the writers erred in telling "about" what was going on instead of making the subject come alive.

For example, a woman wrote a travel article about a tour she'd taken, a "Spooks Tour of Europe," visiting famous haunted houses. The article should have been as exciting as the tour itself. It wasn't. Why not?

She began reading her piece aloud: "We had a thrilling time, an afternoon of thrills and chills. Two of our group performed credibly in demonstrating automatic writing. There was a series of surprising messages from the spirit world . . ." on and on to the very end.

Questions started flying from listeners: "What caused the thrills and chills?" "How did the automatic writing come through?" "How did you receive 'messages from the spirit world'?"

Others asked: "What made the room scary, exactly what did it look like?" "How did the medium communicate with ghosts?" "How was the writing made to appear, and what was so 'surprising' about the messages?"

And finally: "What actually happened from minute to minute that made you, the writer, feel thrilled and chilled? As the listener or reader, I didn't feel any thrills and chills. *What really took place?*"

The author admitted, "I goofed. I thought I was taking the reader on the tour. But now I realize that I was just telling tediously 'about' what happened, rather than re-creating the actuality in full dimension. I'll rewrite to bring readers *into the scene*, so they feel what was actually occurring, thus experiencing the chills and thrills exactly as I did."

I checked with her later. She reported happily that the re-written article was bought and run by a travel magazine. You can write and sell similarly when you make your writing *come alive*.

HOW TO REEDIT TO MAKE HAPPENINGS COME ALIVE

The woman who wrote the much criticized travel article, noted in the preceding section, was a neighbor and friend. She told me after the group disbanded and before she made the sale, "I realize that my writing was inadequate. But I'm not sure how to make what happened on the Spooks Tour come alive."

I took her manuscript and flipped through it, then said, "Here's a specific example: You wrote, 'We viewed a film which showed a priest who had stigmata on his palms from which blood flowed.' "

She nodded, frowning, "Yes. I'll admit that's pretty static."

I went on, "When you described the scene to us over coffee soon after you returned from the tour, you were full of excitement. As I recall, you said something like, 'This tall, bony priest had a face like a hollowed skull. He stretched out long, skeleton-thin arms—and suddenly I shook with fear. I saw blood flowing from wounds in the palms of his claw-like hands. He laid them on the forehead of a crippled child, lifted them away, and there was a red smear on the pale skin.' "

Her eyes had widened in understanding. I explained, "When you said that, I was there, *I saw him, too!* You took us along right with you. That conveyed thrills and chills to us."

"I see what you mean," she agreed.

"You were able to *say* it," I finished, "now *write it.*"

An important added tip there: Often by rereading aloud what you wrote, you can discern that you missed the mark. Then you can rewrite to convey to yourself as the reader what you wanted to get across as the writer but failed the first time.

DO . . . BUT DON'T OVERDO

When you restudy the piece you've "finished," as the writer did in the preceding instance, keep this caution in mind: *When you rewrite, don't overwrite.*

At a meeting of a large group of professional magazine writers, a thoroughly experienced author said, "An editor called me in about an article I'd submitted. She said she liked it but that it needed certain rewriting and additions. She gave me a general idea of what she wanted, and I agreed to revise."

He continued with a grimace, "As she was explaining, I'd realized she was fully on target. I dug in hard, and after my fourteenth rewrite, I felt that the piece was finally shaped up perfectly. But the editor didn't agree. She said, 'Now you've *overpowered* the original idea. You've buried the dramatic impact of the essential message under too much unnecessary detail.' "

With a shrug, he continued, "She was right again. I cut and stitched and finally got the okay."

I read the observation on this recurring problem by a noted author: "Several years of syntax polishing might produce a hymn to literacy, but all too often the initial dynamic vulgarity is lost."

How can you avoid overwriting? Primarily your taste and ability at self-criticism can determine that. The quality improves with extended writing and experience. Again, I manage that successfully most of the time this way (as I emphasize repeatedly):

I put my written draft away for days or a week or more. Then I approach the project fresh, as if I'm a brand-new reader who hasn't seen it before. I find usually, as you will, that flaws tend to surface clearly with this fresh perspective.

Warning: Don't let this happen to you. This instance, which may seem extreme, provides another guideline: An attorney once told me, "I've written enough to fill at least forty books, in the form of briefs. It'll be a cinch to write a best-selling book when I retire." His assistant confided that the attorney's habit was to dictate a brief to her. She'd put it through the word processor, print it out. "He'd make changes on every printout, even dozens of successive printouts, finally stopping only when he had to rush off to a meeting or court appearance."

When he retired, he bought a word processor, wrote the first chapter of his book. Then he rewrote . . . and rewrote . . . and rewrote ceaselessly. Without a deadline, he couldn't finish, gave up disgustedly. (I suggested that he see a therapist.) To be a selling writer, realize that "enough is plenty, too much is a pride" and a dead-end writing block.

ERNEST HEMINGWAY'S FOUR RULES FOR WRITING

A fine journalist and nonfiction writer, as well as a superb novelist, Ernest Hemingway was handed a style sheet with four basic rules when he became a cub reporter on the *Kansas City Star*. Note them well:

Use short sentences.

Use short first paragraphs.

Use vigorous English.

Be positive, not negative.

He said in an interview twenty-three years later, "Those were the best rules I ever learned in the business of writing. I've never forgotten them. No one with any talent, who feels and writes truly about the thing he is trying to say, can fail to write well if he abides by them."

I typed those four rules on a small card which I keep handy near my typewriter. I try to follow them. Think about them for yourself.

THOREAU'S ADVICE: "SIMPLIFY! SIMPLIFY! SIMPLIFY!"

Many beginning writers believe that they will impress editors and readers most by using complicated sentences, multisyllabic words, intricate phrases. Not so. If your writing makes editors and other readers stumble, very often they won't even bother to pick themselves up and read further. Being creative in your writing doesn't mean being complex or clever or impressively "intellectual."

Nor does being simple in your writing mean being stupid or unintellectual in any sense. The prime purpose in writing to sell is to reach out intimately to the reader, to *communicate*. If you ever tempt yourself to write elaborately in order to impress people with "how smart I am," just visualize someone (you've met him) who tries to demonstrate his superiority by talking over the heads of others.

When I emphasized the value of simple writing to a class recently, a student called out happily, "That's wonderful—simple is easiest." "No," I asserted, "simple is hardest. You simplify by going back over your manuscript again and again, cutting unneeded phrases, substituting a short, vigorous word for a complicated, multisyllablic one, smoothing, clarifying."

"Simple" isn't new. Close to two centuries ago, author C. C. Colton stated: "The writer does the most, who gives his readers the *most* knowledge, and takes from him the *least* time."

You'll find it simplest to sell your work when you write simply and clearly.

LISTEN TO WHAT YOU WRITE

I find the following simple activity essential in order to be as certain as possible that my writing *connects*, is not just a lot of wandering and self-pleasing words on paper. To reach readers most clearly and helpfully, your words must "talk" with them in the way they "hear" best and profit most. Readers often, perhaps usually, *hear* printed words more accurately than the author, who is focused primarily on the act of writing.

So, routinely, after I finish a page or segment, *I listen to what I've written by reading the words aloud to myself.* In using conversations and quotes in nonfiction—as in presenting case histories where individuals interviewed have spoken disjointedly—it's especially vital to reread the written sentences aloud, then clarify if necessary.

Try it—I believe you'll be surprised and delighted that you can hear and amend stiff, awkward phrases that may appear understandable on the printed page but sound artificial, phony, confusing to the ear. Your eye (in effect your "inner ear") often cannot catch mannered nuances which tend to creep in and impede interested, involved reading. Such stiff phrases are detected by your listening ear, and corrected.

We've all heard people remark, upon reading a moving piece of nonfiction: "Well said." Of course that means *well written.* It's significant that the reader meant, in effect: "It talked to me."

Reread the page you wrote most recently. Then decide whether the reading-out-loud stratagem works for you. It helps me make my writing more salable—why not yours?

Side Comment:

Controversy recurs about whether or not nonfiction writers must provide any conversations and quotes exactly as spoken, in total detail. If you've ever taped talk in a living room group without the individuals being aware, you've undoubtedly been shocked by the amount of meandering, even incoherent chatter. You'd lose your readers if you were conveying the talk precisely as recorded instead of editing to convey the true essence clearly, interestingly.

I *don't* consider it permissible, however, to concoct scenes and discourse which never occurred at all unless you label the writing as "fiction." You can get yourself and editors and publishers in trouble if you fake what you depict as factual.

USE DIALOGUE AND
QUOTES WHERE FITTING

It's an asset, I find, in selling nonfiction pieces and books to season them with conversation, dialogue, quotes, where they fit and pull readers along. People like to eavesdrop, to *listen in* to what others are saying. Just the "look" of quotes and conversation on the printed page—or repeating people's actual words in other media—often helps to get writing published.

Typically, editors have affirmed to me—"Readers become more involved when you lead them to 'listen' and thus *experience for themselves* exactly what is going on, instead of learning *about* it from a third party, the writer. They'll keep reading more eagerly, especially if they note more personal conversation coming up ahead."

Don't drag in conversation and quotes awkwardly or meaninglessly, but they can be valuable extra writing tools. Use "live talk" when it fits, enlightens, and enriches the basic theme. If you're not using actual or edited words of the speaker, make that clear. It's easy to do fairly. Note how, by introducing the preceding paragraph with "typically," the words reported are clearly a distillation of the comments of a number of editors.

Another means, one of many you can create and use: "I've often heard comments like this from headache sufferers: 'My first warning is a piercing pain in one temple. . . .' " It's definitely valid to condense in order to get the helpful point across.

Another example: In *The Delicious Quick-Trim Diet* book, to make the point that dieters must be realistic and not deceive themselves or others, I condensed a ten-minute conversation, quoting only the few meaningful words spoken:

> *I met a charming, plump woman at a dinner party. I found Anne bright and witty. She told me at one point, "I bought your latest diet book." I smiled and said, "Thanks." She went on, "Obviously I didn't lose weight." I shrugged, "Too bad." After a pause, she touched my arm apologetically and said, "I never went on the diet. . . ."*

Used to make a point intimately and helpfully for the reader, conversational quotes can often be far more compelling and instructive reading than dry "lecturing." Keep the possibility in mind to animate and invigorate your nonfiction writing.

USE PHOTOS AND ILLUSTRATIONS

Some professionals disagree with me on this, but I've proved, through payoff results, that including applicable and illuminating illustrative and photographic material with certain proposals and submissions can help make the sale. No, you don't have to be an artist or illustrator or photographer. I use whatever I can find, or photocopy, or even draw crudely myself. I trust the editor's intelligence to comprehend even rough illustrative material. That has worked for me, as it can for you.

For example, in writing about sex for the mass reader, I wanted the proposal to demonstrate clearly for the editor how specific pelvic area exercises can increase a woman's sexual gratification (also her partner's). I didn't think that the written details alone would demonstrate well enough to the editor or potential readers just how the exercises affect the involved muscles beneficially. Examination of medical manuals turned up a lucid diagram which provided perfect understanding. I made a photocopy and taped it on the proposal. A similar picture was then used in our book.

The all-important point is that you must think through what the editor needs to know about your submission *before* making the offering. Of course, many subjects don't need illustrating, but for articles in differing areas, I've dug until I found photos which were enough like suggested illustrations to include. It didn't matter that they wouldn't be the actual pictures to be used with the final manuscript.

For a travel article about mating African animals, I attached blurry snapshots we'd taken on a photo safari. The pictures weren't used, but the article was. The editor told me later that the unique snapshots caught her attention and led to the acceptance of the piece.

If you're an excellent photographer or illustrator, as well as writer, use those talents in making your submissions and presentations as vivid, meaningful, and eye-catching as possible (but don't get fancy or too elaborate!). Employ your ingenuity to arouse added interest and *prevent* turndowns that could be triggered by not conveying clear understanding and impact.

CONSIDER SUBHEADS TO FEED READERS DIGESTIBLE PORTIONS

Picture yourself sitting down at a restaurant dining table to be served a large full-course meal. Suddenly waiters appear and pile up all the courses before you at once—appetizers, soup, entrée, salad, dessert, coffee. You're stunned by the mass of food besieging you, bewildered about what to tackle first. You're overwhelmed, perhaps losing your appetite. . . .

That tends to happen to many readers who view a mass of solid printed type—almost a barrier blocking them. Notice how most publications, especially those with large circulations, usually break up nonfiction matter particularly into digestible portions—primarily with subheads that highlight the promise of interest, information, entertainment.

Realize again that the editor is a *reader!* Strive to capture his/her attention and involvement in your proposal through subheads, categories, appetizing capsules.

Example of a proposal that scored: At the beginning of my free-lance career, I offered a top women's magazine an article on headaches. That's an important but not unusual subject, so I consciously guarded against the response, "It's been done before." So many articles have been published about headaches that I aimed for something more inviting that would promise *more*— sound, practical instructions to help prevent and cure headaches.

First, I had to avoid the impression that my writing would consist of generalizations or trite discussions "about" headaches. Extensive and intensive research and interviews with various medical experts (even the head of a team of dentists) produced this title and subheads which formed the backbone of the brief but detailed proposal:

10 WAYS TO FIGHT HEADACHES
Sound, practical advice on WHAT STEPS TO TAKE to
help prevent and cure headaches . . .

Every person afflicted with headaches can take new hope for relief. Dr. Arnold P. Friedman, physician in charge at the famed Headache Unit at Montefiore Hospital and Medical Center in New York, says:

1. KEEP A RECORD of Your Headaches, to Help Prevent Them.
2. RELIEVE FEARS with a Special Medical Examination.
3. Have EVERY POSSIBLE HEADACHE CAUSE Checked Out.
4. Heed Your PERSONAL HEADACHE TRIGGERS.
5. Take QUICK ACTION.
6. USE APPROVED DRUGS Speedily and Sensibly.
7. Employ Every Possible SOUND RELIEF MEASURE.
8. EXAMINE YOUR CHARACTER to Help Block Headaches.
9. Improve Your Ways of WORKING, THINKING, LIVING.
10. Get into TOP PHYSICAL CONDITION and STAY FIT.

In my proposal, every subhead was followed by brief listings of specific instructions on how to "Keep a Record," and similarly for all other divisions. My *personal* experiences as a longtime headache sufferer—and what I'd learned from them to make me headache-free now—were included. The editor okayed the presentation instantly for a feature article which pulled exceptional reader response.

Aside from the subhead construction suggested, this point is crucially significant for you: I devoted lots of time and energy *in advance,* with no assurance that my piece would sell, to make a clear, solid, understandable presentation. Many beginners resist such effort. I still take the risks. So what if the payoff isn't there every time? In the trying, I learn a lot. So will you.

GET TO THE HEART
OF THE MATTER FAST!

Watch out for the common mistake of piling up a lot of "garbage"—that is, unneeded and unwanted matter—at the start of your article or book. Get right to the heart of what readers want and need to know.

Always check back over your first paragraph, and a few more, to see whether they could be eliminated as unclear, unhelpful, and therefore not only unnecessary but a turnoff for the reader.

I check back this way again and again with everything I write. More than half the time, I cut out the first paragraph in an article and much of the opening of a book manuscript. Study what you write this way; chances are you'll cut some, and you'll sell more.

Book example: A friend gave me a copy of his first published book, coauthored with a physician. I congratulated him and opened to the first pages. Here's what blocked me immediately:

- A page of "Special Acknowledgements" to "special individuals who have helped tremendously with this book."
- Seven pages of mentions and thanks to people who had "assisted in some way"—laboratory workers, scientists who had done research on the subject, papers from which data was used, on and on.
- Two pages of "Foreword" by a noted doctor who gave the physician-coauthor a long-winded, tiresome pat on the back.
- Nine pages of "Introduction" covering unhelpful, self-serving personal experiences which had led the doctor to work on the book.

Finally, nineteen pages after the opening of the book, the content, which presumably would inform and help the reader with enlightening information, began. I asked my writer friend,

"Why all this stuff up front before you get going to serve the reader?"

"The doctor insisted on it," he said. "I didn't want it. The publisher was against it. But the man is a medical big shot. He insisted that all this stuff stay in—or else no book. So we went along."

I wished him success as I predicted to myself that the book would fail. It did. While all that blockage salved the doctor's ego, it turned readers away. (Most of it should have been eliminated or placed in back of the book.)

Remove roadblocks to the heart of what matters to readers and editors *before* they come down the road to your writing—lest they stop and turn away instead of going your way.

HOW CAN I DEVELOP A "WRITING STYLE"?

I'm glad you asked that question again, friend. Answer: The most efficient approach in developing a "writing style" is this: *Don't waste time trying!* Devote your energy instead to conveying truth, help, vivid description, inspiration, whatever your aim is in reaching out and *bringing meaning alive* for your readers. Your personal way of writing best (your "writing style") will evolve naturally *through the creative act of writing* (nonfiction or fiction).

If you let your mind veer off to the "style" of what you're writing, artificiality creeps in. Just write what you have to say in the forthright way that suits you best. "Forthright" does *not* mean "cut-and-dried." Your writing can be colorful, amusing, elevating—just about anything that reaches and moves your readers effectively for their benefit, interest, and perhaps entertainment.

I commend to you William Strunk's assertion in his worthy book *The Elements of Style:* "All writing is communication; creative writing is communication through revelation." Write to *communicate,* and you will *reveal*—that is an essential of style.

Honored nonfiction author John McPhee's writing style is of-

ten centered on bringing people and places to full-dimensional
life, as in a long piece about doctors practicing in rural Maine:

> *Through the door next comes a twenty-five-year-old female
> who is pregnant, tall, and flourishingly good-looking, and
> weighs a hundred and ninety-seven pounds . . . Five weeks
> to go. The doctor listens in with a stethoscope and hears
> sounds of a warpath Indian drum.*

A writer friend says that my writing style is centered on "the
you connection"—thrusting clearly, simply, swiftly to the reader's self-interest. I agree. That's what developed, but I never
thought of contriving a style, just how to reach the reader best.
He selected the following bit from my coauthored book *"Doctor,
Make Me Beautiful!"* as an example of "you" style:

> *How "necessary" is cosmetic surgery? That blunt question
> is a very personal one, and will be answered just as candid-
> ly for you. This is not just a book "about" cosmetic surgery,
> but written specifically to help solve your personal problems
> and concerns.*

Clearly, there are as many writing styles as there are individual writers. Don't worry about *style*. Do focus on using words,
phrases, sentences that get people to *read and keep reading*.
That's what will make sales for you. Then, suddenly, you'll discover happily that you have a successful writing style without
even being aware of its having evolved.

SIX CHECKPOINTS: TURN INTERVIEWS INTO SALABLE SCRIPTS

Interviews provided one of my first writing sales, and they can
do the same for you. As an unpaid high school reporter for the
Paterson (New Jersey) *Evening News*, finally I won a free-lance
assignment to interview a local theater headliner, orchestra leader Vincent Lopez. When I received a check, I realized that I'd collected on someone else's wise and witty remarks—a definite writing plus.

You can cash in on written interviews more than ever, since this is the age of the celebrity. Because people want to read about "stars," editors fill the demand. Here are simple checkpoints for arranging, writing, selling interview pieces:

1. Create interview opportunities. Be alert for interview possibilities in your area. What personalities live nearby, are visiting, performing, on a lecture tour, passing through? Track down how to reach them—every writer must be part detective when necessary. You can make the interview the basis of the entire piece, or just a part adding to the whole, as in quoting a number of doctors in a health article.

2. Get an editorial commitment if possible. If there's time, check with the local newspaper and with magazines, other publications, to get an assignment—even an agreement such as, "We'll buy it if we like your manuscript." That enables you to say, "I'm writing on spec for so-and-so." Telling the interviewee or representative that you're assigned opens the door readily. Otherwise, radiate confidence as a free-lancer that you'll get the interview published; it's not unusual for a piece to run a year or more later.

3. Arrange the interview appointment. A phone call is the quickest way to an interview. If there's time, you can send a provocative note, then follow by phone to set details. Your way is eased because it's flattering to be interviewed, an ego trip regardless of the status of the interviewer (even when I was a high school student).

4. Be prepared with outline and questions. Know exactly what the interview will cover—it's vital to *plan ahead*. Research the subject ahead of time. A well-known nonfiction writer phoned me (as simple as opening the phone book), wanted to include me in a series on "Making It After Forty" (I'm really twenty-nine). She followed with a letter listing ten questions to consider ahead of time before the arranged phone call. Makes it easier for both parties.

5. Keep the interview as compact, clear, and brief as possible. Use tape or take notes—up to you and the interviewee. Never record without permission. If asked for a copy of your script to check facts beforehand, use your judgment to fit each instance.

   6. Write the interview as the reader. Again, what does the reader want most to know? Use colorful anecdotes, descriptions—whatever adds up to most compelling, informative, entertaining reading. Make the subject and the person come alive! Include photos, illustrations, if they'll help make the sale. Keep the interview moving, interesting, fun for all involved—and you should have a most salable piece.

HOW NOT *TO WRITE OR EPISTOLIZE OR CONFIGURATE*

My ways-that-work repeatedly emphasize the need for simplicity and clarity in nonfiction writing that sells. Here's a contrary, exaggerated example which actually appeared in a printed notice used in the offices of a mammoth corporation:

> *Meetings on equipment acceptance provide a severe test of our synchronized organizational parallel reciprocal monitored time-phased capability.*

   How far do you think the author of that would get as a selling nonfiction writer?
   I commend to you again . . . and again . . . and again . . . Thoreau's exhortation framed on my office wall as a constant reminder:
   Simplify! Simplify! Simplify!

SEND A MESS . . . LOSE A SALE

This should not need saying, but it must be stated: Don't ever send a messy manuscript. If you do, all your writing time and effort will be wasted. *Editors won't read it.* Always wind up with clean, easy-to-read typed sheets, double-spaced, on 16-lb. or 20-lb. white paper (never tissue).

Don't ever get careless and send a mess because you become fed up with rewriting and retyping repeatedly. Don't mail or deliver the pages in hard-to-read form, dirtied, smudged, with confusing cross-outs and write-ins. Take it from any editor: You might as well save the postage and toss the sheets into the wastebasket.

I'm sorry if that sounds harsh and brutal, but your writing deserves the right to be seen at its cleanest and clearest, or shouldn't have been created in the first place. *I want you to sell—* and you will!

THE ESSENTIAL IN EVERYTHING YOU WRITE

Never forget this fundamental necessity as you write, underscored in an important publisher meeting:

About twenty people—publishing executives, editors, marketing, sales, promotion and publicity people—discussed for a couple of hours the launching of *The Complete Scarsdale Medical Diet.* As excellent promotional plans emerged and the session was ending, I raised my voice, "I must add something no one has mentioned: Even if I must say so myself, *this is fine writing—it's a damned good book!"*

In the stunned silence, brilliant editorial head Marc Jaffe smiled broadly and clapped—alone. Oscar Dystel, the preeminent bookman who brought Bantam from near collapse to towering number one, said bluntly: "Of course, we expect fine writing from you—that goes without saying."

The bottom line always: *Fine writing* . . . without it there'd be no articles, no books. To succeed, you must never let down, never submit anything that isn't the best you can possibly do.

Chapter Eight

TO SELL, THINK LIKE AN EDITOR

"Think like an editor." I've recommended that repeatedly to struggling writers trying to turn the key that unlocks and opens the editor's mind—to result in acceptance rather than rejection. Justifiably you ask, "How does an editor think?" Each editor is an individual with varying thought processes, personal likes and dislikes. One thing each has in common necessarily is this: *grabbing, reaching, satisfying most readers.* Here are more specifically practicable, basic checkpoints for success in grabbing, reaching, satisfying *editors* so they buy your offerings.

MANUSCRIPT REJECTED? TRY TURNING IT AROUND

Perhaps it will help you, as it does me, to talk with other writers (as you and I are doing now). About a dozen of us meet for lunch every six weeks or so—whenever one calls others and says, "I need a 'fix' of comfort and hope." At one such get-together, I admitted, "A month ago, my presentation for my twenty-ninth book was rejected, although I felt sure of landing a contract."

"That must have hurt terribly," Marlene said. "After all those books, I thought you had it made."

"Nobody ever has it made," I stated flatly. "Rejections are a fact of writing life one must accept, or quit."

"So," Peter asked, "how did you handle the rejection?"

"I studied my presentation thoroughly to discover *why* it was turned down," I explained. "On the second day of reexamination, I suddenly sighted my stupid mistake: I'd emphasized the promise of the book instead of the *unique self-help method itself*. I turned the presentation around almost completely. The second publisher phoned me yesterday with an enthusiastic okay."

"You mean," Vicki asked, "that just by turning the theme around, you changed a turndown into a sale?"

"That simple turnaround did it," I emphasized to them, and now to you. "Editors rarely have time to analyze a manuscript if it doesn't hit them immediately as being desirable. ***You must be the detective yourself.*** You must track down the fatal flaw that led to rejection, then change it to *earn* acceptance instead of rejection."

Months later, I ran into the editor who had vetoed the idea. I told her about the theme turnaround. She erupted, "Damn! If you'd done that in the first place, we'd have grabbed the book."

Three words that have proved invaluable to me, not always but often: ***Turn it around!*** Try that on your own rejected manuscripts. Hard work, but worth it.

Transform Complaining into Being Constructive

Upon receiving a rejection, the immediate temptation is to put down the editor: "She doesn't know anything good when she reads it . . . she only goes for writers she knows, her buddies . . . the magazine is in a rut, they don't want anything new, fresh, original. . . ."

That's fruitless self-indulgence, isn't it? As a professional now or to be, realize that it's a waste of time and energy you could be using to turn failure into success. The act of knuckling down instead of knuckling under often distinguishes pro from amateur.

I suggest strongly that instead of reacting negatively by wailing that "the editor is wrong," you turn it around and admit: "Maybe the editor is *right*." I believe that I grew up as a writer when I switched to that constructive attitude.

Try it, say it aloud: ***"Maybe the editor is right."*** The next giant step is: "If the editor is right, then the constructive course is to recheck and rewrite to make my manuscript *right!*"

A gutsy writer friend whose work is selling but also getting some rejections (don't we all?) uses this system which you might try: "When I open the mail and find a rejection, I race into the kitchen and set the oven timer for ten minutes of feeling sorry for myself. As soon as the timer rings, I throw off the gloom and doom. I grab the rejected manuscript, read it carefully, then work it over to *make it right.*"

Focus on
"the Kindest Cuts of All"

The "unkindest cut of all" was Shakespeare's phrase for the stabbing of Caesar—but intelligent cutting can be vital in making a rejected manuscript salable. Often overlooked, a prime reason for rejections in this: packing too many unnecessary and therefore burdensome details into an article. Consider this point very attentively.

If you don't discipline your writing intelligently, you may lose out without realizing why. Just recently, a weary mass-magazine editor told me over drinks after a difficult day, "Heaven save me from overwritten articles that tell readers, *and me,* 'more than we care to know.' "

Example: A talented beginning writer wrote a piece about the inner workings of a hotel. Then she complained to me, "I put in weeks of research, interviewed hotel managers, dining room captains, bartenders, waitresses, bellmen, the works—since an editor had responded encouragingly to my inquiry on the subject." She sighed. "I knocked myself out writing the lengthy article. What happened when I sent it in? Back came a rejection note on which was scrawled by hand, 'Good stuff here, but too heavy for us.' It sure is discouraging."

I reviewed her manuscript, along with a batch of others by an adult writing group. I duplicated her pages on my little copier, then marked them. I found myself crossing out huge chunks of detailed description. Returning the sheets to her, I pointed out, "I cut your manuscript in half, down to about 3,000 words instead of your original 6,000. See what you think, trying to be objective as you reread."

Clearly shocked, she wailed, "After all my tough, time-consuming work. . . ."

I went on, "Excellent material here, but just too much of a good thing. I suggest that you smooth it out, make essential cuts, and I think it'll sell. It's up to you. Actually, you should have reviewed the result thoroughly and made such deletions yourself before submitting."

She left, obviously disheartened that she'd been advised to sacrifice some of her precious words and sentences. Apparently, she had second thoughts later. She cut about 40 percent and sold the truncated article to another publication. She wrote to me, "Thanks for your cutting remarks. . . ."

Consider such honest and often brutal self-editing for your own efforts. Like removing calories from a raw steak, trim off the fat. My 2,000-word articles usually bulk up to 4,000 to 6,000 words in the first drafts. But I rarely waste the excess words. You can do as I do: *Save what you cut for use in follow-up pieces.*

RECHECK EVERY SENTENCE YOU WRITE

Whatever the subject, make sure that every sentence you write provides helpful information. That becomes relatively easy when you write as the *reader*. That can unify all subjects for you, since you're functioning as a *people* writer, caring about the reader's self-interest, avoiding writer's self-indulgence.

Example: In writing a book on physical fitness, my M.D. co-author wanted to include details about past body development through the centuries. "Absolutely not," I insisted. "Our readers don't care about the *history* of fitness. Their driving aim is to build a better body, improve circulation, endurance, robust health, and vigor."

The physician suggested further that we should insert some "amusing patient anecdotes." I explained, "Funny stories that make a point to help readers attain the fitness they want—yes. Amusing but meaningful case histories—sure. Comical yarns that simply entertain—no."

I reread every manuscript page repeatedly, crossing out ruthlessly any line that didn't help readers achieve their personal desired goal—the same reason why *you're* reading this. Beautifully crafted phrases, cute twists that say "how clever I am"—*out they go*. While eliminating such "precious" words may bruise your ego, leaving them in will reduce your chances to sell.

Review . . . to Transform
Generalities into Specifics

Perhaps the one most effective way I've found to change a rejected manuscript into a salable one is this: ***Transform generalities into specifics.*** Right now, reexamine one or more of your rejected manuscripts—or apply this recommendation to a piece you're planning to write.

Check carefully in the manuscript that failed to get published. Did you *generalize*—that is, did you present a vague discussion of the subject, rather than specific information, useful facts, readily available information and help to your readers? Beating about the bush instead of getting down to earth comprises one of the most common faults of nonfiction writing that gets turned down instead of accepted and published.

Here's just one specific (yes, specific) example: Like many other authors from the beginning of time, I wanted to convey to readers the importance and essence of *living happily*. I outlined a book "about" happiness. Vague, general, blue-sky stuff. My proposal was spurned repeatedly with record speed—and deservedly so.

Instead of castigating editors, I analyzed . . . Why all the resounding nos from editors and publishers? Because I'd left out the specifics, the "hows" to apply in order to gain maximum happiness. I started over, developed a step-by-step listing of detailed, usable aids. The first editor who saw my new "Conscious Happiness" presentation for the book grabbed it. Title: *Conscious Happiness . . . How to Get the Most out of Living*.

You're probably wondering, "How can one solidify a subject as ephemeral as *happiness* into how-to specifics?" Here's the *specific* chapter listing that demonstrates exactly how the writer can help the reader point by point:

1. What Conscious Happiness Can MEAN FOR YOU
2. WHAT IS True Conscious Happiness?
3. YOUR APPROACH to Conscious Happiness
4. LIVING "the Glorious Life That is Within You"
5. Gaining New AWARENESS
6. Appreciating and Stengthening Your INDIVIDUALITY
7. Self-Quiz: Seeking and Finding YOUR PERSONAL TRUTH
8. DOING What You Want to Do
9. Setting and Reaching Your MOST FULFILLING GOAL
10. Recognizing and Developing Your CREATIVITY
11. The Joys of WORK and ACHIEVEMENT
12. How You Can Gain Increased OPTIMISM, ENTHUSI-ASM, HUMOR
13. GIVING LOVE AND FRIENDSHIP—Helping Others and Yourself
14. FINDING INNER PEACE—Rewards from Beauty and the Arts

So simple: Avoid the unspecific, undetailed, uninformative generalities which help no one. Instead, on the same subject, *convey usable, valuable specifics that will enrich readers*. You'll multiply your chances extraordinarily to make the sale!

RESPECT, BUT DON'T RELY ON EDITORS' REJECTIONS

As a help to you in enduring and overcoming rejections, here's more proof that editors and publishers are not infallible. These are only a few of many actual turndowns:

- "I'm sorry . . . but you just don't know how to use the English language." An editor's comment advising Rudyard Kipling that his writing would never be welcome.
- "You're the only damn fool in New York who would publish it." One leading publisher's comment to another on his deci-

sion to accept William Faulkner's *The Sound and the Fury*.
- ■ "[Your book was rejected here] because it had no reader interest." A noted British publisher's turndown of Frederick Forsyth's *The Day of the Jackal*.

You should now feel fortified and encouraged. Just because your offering may be rejected doesn't necessarily mean that it's not publishable. I urge you to reexamine a rejected manuscript thoroughly. Try to regard it from the *reader's* viewpoint, not just with your necessarily biased focus as the writer. Rewrite the offering if you conclude that revision is needed. But if you're convinced that the manuscript merits publication, submit it again . . . and again and again, if required.

A case in point: A writer who was at last starting to sell told me, "I wrote a short article that I thought would be a sure sale to X magazine. Quick rejection. I sent it on its rounds while I kept writing other stuff. After six months, I decided to try X magazine again. Instant acceptance. Later I asked the editor why it was rejected before. He said, 'Could be any of many reasons. Maybe we'd just run a piece on that subject. Furthermore, editors change—I've only been here a month.' "

That's the way things are. It's almost like a revolving door as editors change at book publishers. It's less so, but still a fact of publishing life at magazines, too. Editor turnover can help you or hurt you. Keep in mind that one editor's dislike may be another's delight. Keep at it. I never stop trying. Well, hardly ever.

WRITE HUMOR AND "LAUGH ALL THE WAY TO THE BANK"

Humor writing is one of the most difficult categories to sell, but when you click, you can score sales steadily. Editors warn that your piece must tickle *most* of their readers—that's not easy, since individual reactions vary considerably. On the other hand, editors keep insisting, "We're always looking for good humorous writing." That usually means "writing that makes *me* laugh." Confusing . . . but the bottom line is: *The market exists.*

I've sold much "funny" writing over the years for all media—print, TV, radio. These recommended guidelines can work for you:

Pull your subjects out of daily life and dilemmas. Will Rogers noted: "Everything is funny as long as it happens to somebody else." That "somebody else" is you, too, since you share common experiences. For high salability, pick a subject that's universal—"existing or prevailing everywhere." Keep the happenings possible, then give them an amusing, even far-out twist, something that's at least *almost* "possible." Here are typical farcical topics that have sold:

- "Learning to Use a Stick Shift"
- "Conquering My Answering Machine"
- "Getting Lost in a King-Size Bed"
- "Uncorking Wine Without a Corkscrew"
- "Losing Weight in a Candy Factory"
- "Opening an Unopenable Plastic-Sealed Package"

As an example, "talking to children" would be one common subject from everyday life. No special research or expertise needed. After all, you were a child once. Or weren't you? So—what humorous twists occur to you? Play with the challenge . . . see what you come up with.

Here's how Russell Baker tackled the subject in his syndicated column: "I was never any good talking to children. Even as a child I couldn't get the hang of it. . . ." He notes that when he tried to talk to other children, the only answer he got was a punch in the nose. That's how a humorous piece is born and developed. Take it from there.

Be on the lookout for funny things. A man in front of me on a Fifth Avenue sidewalk raged about a car jammed in solid traffic, barring him from crossing the street. So he opened the car rear door, *walked through the car itself.* Funny? I tied it in with a few other bizarre traffic incidents, real and imagined, sold the piece to a national magazine.

Get subjects from headlines and everyday news stories. That's what many top humorists do. Then twist the essence to make it all ridiculous. For instance, "politics" is funny—yes, tragic, too—but comedy and tragedy aren't far apart. That in itself could be the basis for a humorous piece. No? Consider what many people laugh at: *Someone falling down.* What's funny about someone tripping, falling flat on his face, breaking bones, and almost killing himself? Plenty of readers too will find that hilarious if it's written up comically, not cruelly. You've seen many such pieces in print. Why not yours?

Study the writing of humor geniuses, such as Art Buchwald, Erma Bombeck, Russell Baker. Afraid they're so good that they bar all competition, including you? Just the opposite. They've opened doors wide for others, since they alone can't fill the lucrative popular market they've proved exists. You can't "make up jokes" like them? Take a lesson from Buchwald's syndicated column in tonight's newspaper. As I write this, the front page is dominated by a political convention—that's a giggle already, right? No "jokes" but . . .

Analyze how Buchwald takes off: He begins: "The stage managers [of the convention] are in a tizzy. How do you keep the TV public's attention for four days when the nominations of the President and his Vice President are a sure thing? I went over to campaign headquarters to see what was going on. . . ." The grinning begins.

The rib-tickling twist, obvious but hilariously carried through, is that the usual "anti" demonstrators against the nominees refuse to show up because the convention is too dull. Finally, the convention staff must disguise themselves as violent demonstrators in order to arouse some excitement.

There's the twisted idea, right from the headlines. Try it—grab the headline—and *twist.* You can do it—you're a creative writer, aren't you?

Extreme warning: Apply restraint, don't ha-ha-ha overwrite. I've called on a number of titans to back up my caution. Churchill: "A joke's a very serious thing." Carlyle: "The essence of humor is sensibility"—understanding, restraint, taste. Most significant is the rule of O. W. Holmes: "I never dare to write as funny as I can."

If rejected, submit, submit again. I've learned repeatedly that one editor's judgment of what is meaty, wanted humor is another's idea of thumbs-down smelly fish. When a humor piece comes back, I shoot it right out to another outlet. It may take many submissions, earn comments from some—"Dreadful." But eventually I received a note—"Hilarious!"—and a check. Go to it!

Ten-Word Guide to Using Humor in Nonfiction

Careful use of humor can often be a considerable help in seasoning a nonfiction piece to make it most delicious and digestible for the reader. However, the greatest fault in using humor, affirmed to me by one of the most successful comedy writers, is *overuse.* He passed on to me this Ten-Word Guide for employing humor in nonfiction particularly, quoting the words of O. W. Holmes which I just mentioned: *"I never dare to write as funny as I can."*

The temptation is tremendous to overdo as you throw in "a few laughs" to sparkle up a nonfiction piece. I emphasize this because I've collected rejections for such self-indulgence, as may have happened to you without your realizing it.

In one instance, an editor responded favorably to my proposal for a serious, authoritative article on why people go for horror movies, which was based on an interview with a respected psychologist, plus additional research findings. The piece was intended to inform and also provide the reader with some thrills and chills—the editor's suggestion.

As I wrote, facets of the subject struck me as being funny, so I inserted some humorous highlights. Delighted with the final result of a lot of intensive, serious effort, I sent in the article. It boomeranged back almost by return mail. The editor's turndown read in part: "I enjoyed the piece, but it was too funny to be scary or believable. You missed the mark."

Funny? I reread carefully and was appalled. I'd allowed the comical aspects to take over at critical moments. I'd indulged myself by trying to be "clever," instead of developing the basic theme cleanly, concisely, informatively.

I took the editor's analysis to heart (I urge you to do the same whenever you find an editor's comment on a rejection; otherwise, you must dig out the defects yourself). I sliced out much of the humor, leaving just a few light rays to illuminate and accent the doom and gloom by contrast. When I resubmitted the article with an apology and thanks, the editor bought it.

Please repeat to yourself after me: *"I'll never write as funny as I can."*

SHUN THE "QUICK FIX" IN REWRITING

It will pay you to keep this parallel in mind when revising a manuscript or rewriting to make it salable after a turndown:

I learned this creative fact from my wife, Natalie, a professional artist and art teacher. She has pointed out to me repeatedly that when an artist changes something important in a painting, she or he usually must go over the entire work—eliminating here, adding there, balancing all the elements. *The same is true generally in reworking a manuscript to make it acceptable.*

When you change the beginning of a manuscript, for instance, it may cause a subtle shift of emphasis throughout, which should be checked. If I insert a few new facts or observations, I work to conform to these alterations throughout, or the totality won't get across to the reader with full interest, conviction, help.

Regardless of the extended, demanding work involved, rewriting too little tends to produce artificiality and lack of forward drive and cohesiveness. If the editor skips a beat in reading and judging, continued interest may be lost, along with the chance for being published.

Ask the professionals—they'll affirm that one of the biggest mistakes is to yield to the temptation to give your manuscript a lick and a promise in a hurry. Chances are that you'll wind up blaming the editor again for a lack of perception after another rejection. Never forget it: Haste makes wasted opportunity in the writing game.

Write or Rewrite . . . Then Back Away

Remember this caution (you'll be reminded of this by me from many different slants, because it's so fundamental and essential):

After writing or rewriting intensively, *back away*. Why? Because it's an irrefutable fact that when you've been deeply involved in a work, you tend to lose perspective and judgment.

When you reread your manuscript—short or long—as soon as you finish, it's difficult, almost impossible, to spot errors and flaws. Sure, go over it right away when it's fresh, but then take a pause that releases and refreshes your mind and your clear understanding.

I've made this mistake many times, both with articles and book manuscripts, working chapter by chapter. Following intensive writing, I've been impatient more than once. I haven't always heeded my own admonition to *put the manuscript away for at least a week, preferably weeks*. Then, and only then, are you able to read your own writing again with a cold, clear, objective editorial eye.

In one instance, when I finished a book manuscript, instead of backing away for a while, I read hastily, retyped, and delivered the complete work to my agent. He phoned me two weeks later: "I hate to say this, but your book isn't right yet for submitting to a publisher."

I was jolted—another rejection, in effect. He went on, "Now that you've been away from the writing for a couple of weeks, I want you to reread it as though it's a new book you've just purchased at a store, one you've never seen before. Read it as though you were a reader, and as a judgmental editor—not as the writer. Then come in and we'll discuss it in detail."

I was not happy, but forced myself into a fresh mind-set and began rereading. A few days later, I phoned him: "You're right. The manuscript is teeming with errors usually made by a beginning or unpublished writer. Too much description involving unnecessary details. Too many twists and turns veering away from the main points that the reader needs and wants to learn. It's overwritten, underedited. Back to the drawing board."

By following this course, you can make your writing right, as I did with that book manuscript which turned into a big seller. It's tough to wait and then start all over again, but you'll find that it pays off in tangible rewards.

LEARN TO THINK
AS AN EDITOR THINKS

In preceding segments, you've read and, I trust, absorbed and profited from many of my experienced recommendations about approaching and working with editors, whether you're aiming to sell magazines or book publishers right now. This subject is so crucial to selling that I believe the expansions and additions here are valuable and perhaps essential for you.

How does one think like an editor? You must try to find a way into the editor's head, to feel and think and react as an editor does. Obviously, if you haven't met the editor or even talked with the person on the phone, you don't know what she or he looks like or anything about the individual's character and personality.

Here's how I've always done it: I close my eyes, picture the editor I'm aiming to reach and sell. I form a mental image of the editor's face, usually a woman because most editors in publishing are female. I visualize that individual . . .I become that person . . .and I try to look at *my* manuscript through her eyes and thus to judge her assessment of my offering.

How can I estimate how likely she is to evaluate my manuscript as a publishing possibility? The way I find out, to the best of my ability as a stranger, is this: If she is a magazine editor, I study carefully the last few issues of the publication. I know that the same thinking that chose the articles and features appearing in these issues would apply in selecting or rejecting my offering, since she would be following the same standards.

Yes, I know that no one editor chooses everything in the magazine, but it's a fact that every editor must recommend for purchase what the editorial director and/or editorial board has determined the magazine's readers want. If the readers' desires and interests aren't addressed and satisfied, the publication will lose circulation and eventually go out of business. Realize, therefore, that the editors have more to lose than you have.

The proof to me that the "transference" works is that once I started visualizing the editor, then tried to think as the editor thinks, my percentage of rejections dropped, and my acceptances increased. To apply this effective procedure to *book* editors, examine publishers' lists, as well as books on sale in stores. You'll soon learn that Alfred A. Knopf is more likely to emphasize "literary values" and more weighty nonfiction subjects. Prentice-Hall, on the other hand, goes more for "mass appeal," self-help, how-to nonfiction, engineering and business areas.

Examining and weighing what magazine and book executives choose to publish will provide an avenue into the editors' heads and help you think the way an editor thinks. To apply the editor's viewpoint, ask yourself before making a submission: *"Would I, as editor, buy what I, as writer, am offering?"* The answer will help you score hits instead of misses. There's no doubt about that in my mind, based on my experience in writing and selling.

Be wary of the opinions and criticisms, favorable or adverse, of family, friends, anyone. The only individuals who really count are editors who can *buy* what you write. You could be doing yourself a great disservice by taking a friend's negative opinion which might discourage you about a piece that an editor might like and purchase.

READ YOUR COVERING LETTER THROUGH THE EDITOR'S EYES

Always reread repeatedly your covering letter through the eyes of the editor you're addressing. She, in turn, looks through the *readers'* eyes, asks: "Is this what our readers want?" She may admire the style of your proposal, the unique subject matter and original approach. But she can't buy your article or book if it won't win readers.

An editor of a women's magazine bought a hard-boiled mystery novel because he enjoyed it exceptionally. Checking readership and letters revealed that the selection was a disaster. "Worth trying," he told me ruefully, "but it taught me again to buy what most readers go for, not just because I enjoyed something personally."

Please double-check these essential guideposts for your covering letter:

The first few words must grab the editor's attention. For example, consider this too common beginning: "Herewith is a proposal about an article describing a new development in child health care." Compare with this grabber: "Over five hundred children died unnecessarily last year because . . ." Which opening would you be more likely to read?

Cut out all excess words. Chop the oft-seen "I am sending herewith a proposal" or "You will find herewith a proposal." Even "Here's a proposal," although not a grabber, is less an impediment to reading further. Cut-cut-cut—instead of "at this point in time," simply say "now."

Don't try to impress with sophisticated "literary style." "Destroy" is preferable to "eradicate" . . . "generous" instead of "magnanimous." Just *say* it quickly, clearly—editors look for content, not pretentious writing. Test: Read your letter aloud—to detect and cut complicated words that become stumbling blocks.

Do send a covering letter, even with a one-page proposal. Keep it to one or two short paragraphs which *excite* the editor to read the proposal.

YOU DON'T NEED A REPUTATION TO INTEREST AN EDITOR

It's much tougher in the beginning to get prime interest from an editor, no question about that. Nor is there any question that you *can* interest and sell an editor. You must offer the right, potent idea, a grabber opening in your proposal letter, a convincing presentation (to a magazine or book editor)—you'll sell sooner or later if you just keep writing intelligently.

You learn the practicable ways-that-work in this book. Then *you* have to apply those methods in your approaches. You keep trying again and again until you succeed, as you must and will. You're certainly convinced by now that my how-to recommendations are not theory, but proved directions that lead to earnings from your writing.

You've heard often from doomsayers that "editors won't read unsolicited offerings. You must go through an agent." Innumerable writers, including myself, have proved that such negatives aren't true. Yes, book editors especially will give more attention to a proposal from a reputable agent because they believe that the agent has screened the offering first and eliminated inferior or misdirected material. Many, perhaps more magazine editors, however, prefer to work with a writer at first hand, not through an agent.

It's a fact that the editor who finds a gem in unsolicited proposals gets higher praise for acuteness and enterprise. Editors' reputations have been built on unexpected finds and buys from unknown writers, usually obtained at low cost. I know a book editor who recognized and bought a manuscript rejected by many others which turned into a blockbuster best-seller; his reputation throughout his career rested on recognition by publishers that "he's the editor who bought that astounding blockbuster for peanuts!" Editors too enjoy the thrill of *discovery*.

When I had little standing, and no agent, I wrote a presentation for a gardening book to appeal to kids—not considered a promising publishing project previously. I had never proposed anything for children before. The first publisher rejected it bluntly: "Hopeless. Not a chance." Next try—a brilliant Random House editor phoned me excitedly, "Great creative idea, something different, and your three samples of things and ways to grow are ingenious, real fun for kids."

The very popular *Indoor and Outdoor Grow-It Book* went into many editions, hardcover and trade paperback. I asked my editor whether she bought many unsolicited manuscripts. She said, "Not many, because most aren't good enough. But when we discover a winner, it's a special thrill." I learned that the reader at Random House was given a bonus for detecting the proposal in the mass of material arriving "through the transom" or in the "slush pile" (as unsolicited offerings are usually dubbed).

This is only one of countless such successes by beginning and other writers through the years. You won't be defeated if you refuse to be discouraged, and keep trying indefatigably. Nor will you sell if you don't make the offerings. Keep this marketing fact in mind: Editors are always looking for "something different"— at the same time, it must project high appeal to *many* readers, not just a few.

Follow Up the Slightest Interest by an Editor

If an editor makes any encouraging comment at all about an offering—a few handwritten words on a rejection slip or a brief mention on the phone or in person—follow up as soon as possible with carefully created proposals. Just a month ago, a writer told me that the editor had jotted on the rejection, "Nicely written, but can't use." I asked, "What did you offer next?" "Offer? I just felt good. . . ."

In my earliest tries to be published, I was taken especially by a feature in a top national weekly magazine, paying a lot for brief humorous anecdotes. I sent one which the editor returned with one penciled word: "No." I was delighted—at least he had noticed me. I mailed an offering a week. Finally, my twentieth submission brought a check and a note: "I kept watching and wondering when you would click." As I keep reminding writers, editors are human, too. Editors are among the best people I've ever met.

When an editor likes your work, she or he can do a lot for you. I once asked an executive of M-G-M, "With so many people trying to break into show biz, what makes *one* a star?"

He said thoughtfully, "In many cases, it's because one individual connected with the business believes in that actor or actress—usually not sexual, but a faith in that person's charisma, what-have-you. The insider keeps knocking on doors, talking it up, gets the beginner an opening—then talent has to come through to succeed."

The same can happen for a writer. Usually you have to make it entirely on your own. Nevertheless, if you detect some special interest by an editor or anyone in publication or book publishing, *make the most of the slightest notice of you.*

Act alertly and quickly on any expression by an editor regarding subject matter. More and more, editors at magazines and in book publishing seek to originate their own article and book ideas. That makes sense because they know best what will attract readers of their magazine or book purchasers. They still buy loads of original offerings, but like very much to affect and steer the themes and details of manuscripts.

I've made sales after an editor turned down my presentation, then remarked casually, "I wonder if there might be something in a book on so-and-so—but forget it, probably a lousy idea." You can be sure that if the idea appealed to me at all, I'd be back in short order with an offering stemming from that seemingly offhand comment. Would you?

Specific example: I'd been trying to sell pieces to the editor of a special feature. He sent back a number of my proposals. On the latest turndown he noted that he thought it would be amusing to read about titles of self-help books that would never be written. Within a week, I sent him a listing which he approved instantly. Here are a few of my suggestions:

- *How to Make a Million Dollars by Writing Scare Books About Money*
- *Everything You Always Wanted to Know About Sex and Asked About and Were Sorry You Did*
- *Fanny: Being the True History of a Spot-Reducing Diet*
- *The Joy of Hex: Witchcraft Made Easy*

It's indisputable: If you pass up the slightest possibility, you won't score.

TRY TO TARGET EDITORS' PERSONAL ENTHUSIASMS

This unusual insight can be extremely helpful in making the sale: Try to direct your proposal on a specific subject to an editor who has exceptional interest and enthusiasm in that area. For instance, if your offering is about fitness, your best chance is to reach an editor who's an exercise devotee. Gardening, cooking, diet—seek the editor who is personally excited about those themes.

The eventual editor of one of my diet books was overweight and felt guilty after a weekend of heavy eating. She found my manuscript on her desk Monday morning, she told me later. It grabbed her. She went on the diet, lost over ten pounds by the next editorial meeting. She raved about the book to the others, wouldn't take no for an answer. Sale!

My presentation for *Vigor for Men over 30* was rejected a couple of times, then reached an editor in his midthirties who was an exercise freak. He approved enthusiastically, sold the editorial board. Unfortunately, he took a better job with another publisher just as *Vigor* was coming off the presses. I met with the new editor, a flabby individual, to discuss promotion and publicity. He said, yawning, "I couldn't care less about vigor and fitness. I hate exercise!" That hurt sales.

So . . . you take advantage of good breaks and bear up under bad luck. You make every effort to reach an editor who is an enthusiast. How? If you have an agent, you emphasize that point in advance, since the agent knows the personal interests of editors. If no agent is involved, phone the magazine or publisher (as I did many times), ask to whom a presentation on the particular subject should go.

Another slant: Check subject listings (e.g., "Beauty Editor") in magazines. Similarly, examine books on the same subject as yours, then phone the publisher and get the name of the editor on that book. Send your presentation to him or her. Use your ingenuity to track down the right editor for you. It's a challenging pursuit that pays off.

WORK WITH THE EDITOR IN EVERY POSITIVE WAY

When an editor asks for some rewriting or revisions, I urge you to react positively unless you're *certain* that the proposal or article or book is perfect as is. In any case, don't blow your top or even respond negatively by reflex. The editor is seeking to make your offering better, to make it more acceptable to the magazine or book publisher—and to readers.

On a recent book, the intelligent editor said very gently and carefully, "Samm, we have some suggestions for changes that we think will help the book. I hope you don't mind. . . ." I spoke instantly, "Great, let's make it the best it can be." She smiled and said, "I almost forgot—you're a pro."

Many writers hit the ceiling when an editor suggests or even makes changes in a magazine piece without checking for the writer's approval. I think the writer should always be informed in advance, but if it happens after the fact of publication, I shrug it off. Next time I offer something to that editor, I say quietly that I want to be consulted about any changes. The response has always been, "Fine, no problem."

On a book, the one time an editor made extensive changes in my manuscript (that was before I had any reputation), I was fortunate to catch it before it reached the typographer for galleys. I realized that the young inexperienced editor was, consciously or not, trying to make the book her own. When she refused to reconsider, I went over her head to the editorial director (whom I hadn't met), showed him the marked-up manuscript. He fired the editor on the spot. He went back to the original manuscript and a knowledgeable editor.

Be helpful to your editor in every positive way—she or he can be a powerful aide and force. An enthusiastic editor will exert vital influence on designing the book right, raising the interest of marketing and sales people, striving for maximum promotion, publicity, advertising. The editor can make a crucial difference in the success or failure of your book.

Editors welcome creative, practical ideas for promoting your book, but react strongly and negatively to constant nagging and complaints from writers. Get as much attention as you can for your book, but don't demand or expect too much—that can turn off the editor and publisher completely. Be realistic in realizing that yours is not the only book on the publisher's long list. That insight may be hard to accept, but it's true.

A writer bragged to me that he'd forced the publisher to

change the jacket design of his new book three times. "Then," he boasted, "after the artwork was finished, I made them throw it out and create a new design. I had them over a barrel because they liked the manuscript of my next book." A month later, he said unhappily, "The publisher returned my new manuscript with a flat rejection, no explanation. I don't understand why."

In dealing with editors and publishers, I recommend that you be positive and cooperative. Speak up at any time, courteously and intelligently, always backing your views with sound reasons. Remember that your editor and you share a mutual goal: greatest *sales success for your book* (or for the magazine).

Chapter Nine

HOW TO PRODUCE PROPOSALS THAT SELL ARTICLES

Before presenting a proposal, *think it through.*

Those three words—***think it through***—may be the most important and helpful advice you ever absorbed in creating proposals that result in sales. Usually you read a lot on this subject about preparing and submitting a manuscript, double-spacing on 20-lb. white bond, mailing flat in a large envelope, including a stamped, self-addressed additional envelope, and so on.

But you still don't make the sale . . . right? The primary missing element, affirmed overwhelmingly by editors I've queried, is this: ***The presentation isn't thought through.*** That is, it doesn't convey anything or enough that's fresh and different; furthermore, it doesn't clearly promise exceptional benefits for the reader (and therefore, the editor).

I urge you to read that point again and again. Absorb it in your consciousness before you submit another proposal. First, ***think through*** the entire thrust of your offering and what it embodies in total. Convey explicitly the specific advantage for the reader ***before approaching the editor.***

You'll learn exactly how to do it right in the following ways-that-work. . . .

TRY TO LIMIT YOUR PROPOSAL TO ONE PAGE

It may not always be possible, but it's very desirable to try to keep your proposal on one page, no more. Sure, it takes extra time and work to condense the vital essence of your total idea to that limited space; as Pascal wrote, "I have made this letter rather long only because I've not had time to make it shorter."

I've always found the extra application not only worthwhile but often crucial in having the proposal read. I learned the hard way, as an advertising agency executive. When I sent or handed a proposal to a client, if it was more than one page, even if important decisions about millions of dollars were involved, he'd usually put it aside: "I'll get to it later." Later never came, unless I brought the matter up again. (Weighty long-range plans were exceptions, of course.)

The same frequently happens with editors. If the proposal is longer than one page: "I'll put it aside for now." That's frequently the kiss of death. Editors are generally overburdened and overworked, with too little time for reading something new, despite the best intentions. Realize the danger, too, that if your proposal isn't brief, it can become tedious.

Grant me a pertinent personal anecdote (when I was a young aspiring writer in his class, Dashiell Hammett said, "Authors are permitted to indulge themselves at least once in each manuscript"): As head of an advertising agency, I asked our media director for a brief one-city TV proposal for a product—"Keep it to one page, this client won't read more." Next day, she sent me *three* pages. In a hurry, I rewrote it to a half page, which the client okayed. I showed it to Blanche, asked, "Why couldn't you have done that in the first place?" She replied, "Samm, if I could do that, I'd be getting your salary." She could have done it—if she cared enough. So can you.

THREE-STEP STRUCTURE
FOR EFFECTIVE
PROPOSALS

Reviewing and analyzing a number of my successful magazine article proposals, I found they usually boil down to three structural steps. Consider these carefully. They've helped to build a high batting average in getting approvals:

1. State the subject succinctly.
2. Explain briefly the special values embodied for readers.
3. Show clearly and convincingly how the theme will be conveyed, point by point.

Check the submissions you've made previously against this structure. Have you carried through your proposal impressively according to these three stages? It may pay you to revise those submissions and offer them elsewhere. Think deeply along these lines on your future proposals.

DON'T JUST "PROPOSE"
AN IDEA . . . SPELL IT OUT
IN DETAIL!

Thinking forward, as you must do in planning your writing sales, I deliberated in January about a diet article that would appeal to mass magazines for women as a summer feature. Thinking it through, I realized that—with so many diet articles sprouting all over the place—my proposal had to have special, eye-catching appeal. And my description would have to convey that outstanding power in order to get an acceptance.

So . . . what to offer? It took me several weeks of planning to research and shape up the following proposal:

This brand-new reducing diet—created specifically for presummer slimming—will help women (and men) lose weight with exceptional speed and ease right before swimsuit season:

NEW SPEEDY SUMMER SHAPE-UP DIET . . .
LOSE 10 POUNDS OR MORE IN 2 WEEKS
AS SIMPLE AS A-B-C.

No counting calories. No weighing foods. Everything pre-planned for you. The diet consists of two SELECTION CHARTS . . . one for BREAKFAST . . . the other for LUNCH/ DINNER. Each chart offers three columns: A-B-C.

FOR BREAKFAST: Column A lists juices and fruits. Column B lists eggs, cereal, and so on. Column C lists coffee, tea. Dieter chooses one each from A-B-C—according to personal preference.

For LUNCH AND DINNER: Column A lists a variety of main dishes, poultry, fish, meats. Column B lists a variety of vegetables and salad fixings. Column C lists desserts of fruits, others. Dieter chooses one from A, two from B, one from C . . . plus coffee, tea, or no-sugar carbonated drinks.

BONUS ADDITIONAL TREATS: Bonuses in three columns: A-B-C. BONUS A lists assortment of unlimited beverages. BONUS B lists "anytime" snacks of no-sugar gelatin desserts, raw and cooked cold vegetables, crackers, others. BONUS C lists alcoholic drinks, types and quantities permitted, one a day.

IMPORTANT TIPS: 16 simple guide-tips to help dieter lose weight speedily, pleasantly, easily, and keep dieting.

NO-NOs: 14 preventive guidelines for quick, sure weight loss.

SAMPLE DAY'S MENU: Shows one person's A-B-C and BONUS choices for a day's delicious, satisfying, slimming eating. Choose to satisfy your personal tastes similarly, changing menus daily.

(NOTE TO EDITOR: This safe, sure, 1,200-calorie diet has been checked with an M.D. whose name may be used or not— your decision.)

This brief proposal contained all the basic information the editor needed. She phoned me to check a few details, then made her presentation to the editorial board. She called with the okay and fee offered (satisfactory to me).

Mission accomplished. If my proposal had simply covered

the advantages of a presummer reducing diet, without essential details, I'm certain that it would have been rejected.

The sequence is clear: Start with a clearly appealing idea on whatever the subject may be (certainly not limited to diet). Think through your proposal in detail. Put in the time and effort required to flesh out the concept soundly, solidly. You'll be getting acceptances instead of turndowns.

ADD IRRESISTIBLE FEATURES TO THE BASIC IDEA

Pay close attention to this vital, repeated failing of many proposals. I urge you to note and avoid it in the future: ***Don't stop with the basic idea, which frequently isn't strong enough to make the sale on its own.*** In many instances, although the theme itself may be worthy, it doesn't offer sufficient reader benefits to get the editor's okay.

Your proposal must put across the idea as sufficiently "new" and "different" to attract readers. Then you have to include the specific features which *prove* that your article will help people exceptionally. This precise case history proves it:

Pointing out in a diet proposal that women especially are extremely concerned about putting on pounds and inches, I offered a "holiday diet" to control this weight-gain problem. I provided a few details about the diet itself and was certain I'd get the assignment from the first editor approached.

I fell off my high wire of confidence when a rejection followed: "Nothing new about offering a holiday diet." What to do to make the sale? Instead of indulging myself by muttering about editors' stupidity and shortsightedness (the usual reaction), I considered the reason for the turndown carefully. I realized that this editor was right—I'd have to add irresistible features to the sound basic idea.

I followed through with this revised proposal, including "new irresistible features" added to the original idea:

SUBJECT: 4-STEP BEFORE-AND-AFTER HOLIDAY EATING PLAN

Step One: 7-DAY BEFORE-HOLIDAY DIET—takes off any excess pounds the week *before* the holidays begin.

Step Two: HOLIDAY-WEEK EATING RULES—guides your eating, but many usual dieting restrictions are lifted so you can indulge and enjoy yourself without massive weight gain.

Step Three: LIQUIDS-ONLY ONE-DAY RELIEF DIET— choose one or two nonsuccessive days during holidays to follow this diet to get an eating rest, relieve bloat and discomfort, take off a few pounds quickly.

Step Four: 7-DAY AFTER-HOLDIAY DIET takes off extra pounds and inches quickly; continue diet for second week if necessary.

Result: Anyone can enjoy happier, healthier, more enjoyable and *beautiful-body* holidays with this doctor-approved 4-STEP BEFORE-AND-AFTER HOLIDAY EATING PLAN!

I decided to submit this "4-Step Plan" instead of the previous "Holiday Diet" to the same editor—in spite of the earlier rejection—since I respected her and the magazine highly. Enthusiastic acceptance came within the week. That's the difference possible by adding irresistible features to a good basic idea. You must put in the extra effort and work: You have to *earn* the sale through your powerful, multiple-feature proposal.

Be Creative and Persistent: Make It Better!

Some years ago, a line from a best-selling inspirational book swept the country: *"Every day in every way I'm getting better and better."* The premise was that by repeating that line over and over daily, people couldn't help but feel better about themselves, gain self-confidence, apply more energy. Thus, they would actually *be better* every day in every way.

Whether or not the statement worked is unknown to me, but I assure you that the "make it better" system will boost the selling power of your proposals. Check back to the preceding comments on the Holiday Diet, then proceed in this sequence:

1. Work out the Holiday Diet more effectively . . .

2. *Make it better!* Result: "Before Holiday" Diet added to the other features . . .

3. Don't stop there—*make it even better:* "Holiday-Week Eating Rules" evolve . . .

4. Is that enough? *Try harder:* "One-Day Relief Diet" is added to the other features . . .

5. *Do still better?* Yes: An "After-Holiday Diet" completes the eating plan as "new" and "different."

That did it—made the sale. The clear conclusion is that a writer should never be satisfied with a proposal without attacking it over and over again to make it better, make it the best! Only then should you send out the offering with the strongest possibility of winning an acceptance.

THINK BIG: PROPOSING A SERIES

Think ahead—this is another reminder. And, in addition, it sometimes pays to *think big*, as in this example:

As the year was nearing its end, I focused on thinking ahead to magazine summer issues. Studying publications, I had noted that most of the mass-circulation giants offered advertisers the opportunity to buy sectional subdivisions at lower rates. They could choose from big-city readership, New England, Southern, and so on, fitting their individual product distribution patterns to media selections.

Considering what I might offer with special regional appeal led me to focus on summer gardening. I recalled that when living in New York City, we had special problems trying to grow plants on a terrace seventeen stories up. People with gardens in small enclosed yards, penthouses, rooftops, and window boxes—in any city—encountered similar troubles. Yet I'd never read much in publications about help for city gardeners. A special opportunity for a writer?

You've heard the repeated advice: *"Find a need and fill it."* I'd discovered a common problem, decided to offer a solution. I dug into the subject, drew from my own experiences and knowledge, augmented by questioning many others. In developing a proposal, I found the article expanding beyond the short size usually appearing in sectional editions.

Mulling this over, I realized that the multifaceted subject merited more than one article for greatest aid to concerned readers. I stressed that point in my offering, recommending either a single article (in order not to overreach and perhaps lose out completely) or an entire series. The following is taken right from the proposal:

> OVERALL SERIES TITLE: *Essential Tips for City Gardeners*
>
> JUNE: *Prepare Ahead for Summer Gardening*
>
> JULY: *How to Beat the Heat in Your Garden*
>
> AUGUST: *First-Aid Hints for Midsummer Gardening*
>
> SEPTEMBER: *Boosting Gardening Rewards to Summer's End.*

A few explanatory lines covered subject matter for each successive piece in the series. I wound up with a compact, easy-to-digest proposal on a single sheet. The editorial board went for the series. I was told that they'd have purchased just one "City Gardener" article, but preferred the continuing set once it was outlined so clearly.

Keep this suggestion in mind as a way to multiply your appearances in print . . . and your earnings.

TO SELL A SHORT PIECE, SKIP THE PROPOSAL

Don't become blocked by any strong feeling that you *must* send a proposal to a publication before you can sell the editor anything. From my experience, that doesn't apply to short pieces.

It would appear silly to me as an editor (which I have been) to be queried about a piece which would be a thousand words or fewer about any subject. I've encountered a number of tight-lipped professional writers who assert that they won't write *anything* without an editor's approval and agreed fee beforehand. Bluntly, I don't believe them. I've sent short pieces to various publications over the years, skipping the proposal stage. Some were rejected, most accepted, accompanied by a check which might be smaller or larger than expected. I've taken my chances. Your decision about what course to take is entirely your own.

Typical experience: I heard somewhere that an editor at *Redbook* wanted humorous pieces of universal appeal. I'd noted confusing (to me) titles that often appear for a single episode on a popular half-hour or hour dramatic TV series, such as: "Wild Horses Race over Knobby Knolls". . . "Stars Sparkle. Society Smirks. Why?" Wild! I wrote a thousand words about "Those Wacky TV Titles—What Do They Mean?" The editor bought it.

Suit yourself—your choice to propose or to dispose with the proposal.

PROPOSALS DESIRABLE, BUT NOT ALWAYS A MUST

A proposal makes sense for an article of more than a half-dozen pages for one reason: Particularly with major large-circulation magazines, editors usually won't read a longer manuscript from an unknown writer because of limited time and the pressures of overwork.

A wit contended that the work of a network vice-president is finding a molehill on his desk in the morning and making a mountain of it by day's end. That's not true of editors or most other workers. The biggest problem in publishing and other businesses, in my lifetime experience, is that individuals are so busy trying to handle masses of work piled on them daily that there's little time left to think, to innovate, or simply to pay attention to anything new.

Nevertheless, I've never permitted myself to become discouraged or stymied, nor should you. Keep writing. Keep trying. You'll succeed. For example, before I was a known writer, I was intrigued by the subject of sex in business—who does what to whom and when and what are the consequences.

I started with the heading "SEX IN THE OFFICE? A Report from an Executive." I made a skeleton outline of my main points, then started to flesh it out into a proposal. I found myself writing too much for proposal length and decided, "The hell with it, I'll write the whole damned article—and take my chances." I sent the twelve pages to a national magazine; to my surprise it was accepted immediately!

Three centuries ago, Cervantes wrote, "There is no rule without an exception." I suggest that you consider experienced advice thoroughly, then pursue your personal instincts and initiative.

Chapter Ten

BUILDING PROPOSALS THAT SELL BOOKS

Ready to try a book? You'll need to make a strong proposal. Don't be confused: "Presentation" and "proposal" are interchangeable words, whether you're offering an article or a book or other writing aimed to sell. I stress "presentation" for a book proposal because it must be more solidly constructed than for an article. Building a book presentation, for me, is like creating a blueprint for a skyscraper. You must establish an enduring foundation, then erect the edifice floor upon floor, complete with electrical facilities, plumbing, on and on.

You must be willing and able to put in a tremendous amount of work before you're ready to present practically any book *and sell it.* If you can't or won't invest the time and effort, you're not likely to succeed. There probably are exceptions, but I'm not aware of them, certainly not with any of my thirty published books. *You* are ready to toil for book publication, or you wouldn't be reading this.

Does the quality of the presentation make a buy-or-reject difference? When I started offering books, four were turned down primarily due to inept, unfocused presentations. When I worked each proposal over and over, until they were gripping, clear, orderly, and factually convincing, they were bought. Since many other factors are involved in signing a book, a fine presentation doesn't guarantee getting a contract—but it sure helps.

Worth the great effort? You decide. A book, like a diamond, as I've stressed, is "forever"—or almost. Many authors, like myself, are collecting royalties annually on books they wrote more than twenty years ago. Furthermore, when a book goes out of print and your rights are returned, you can rewrite and bring it up to date, or use the basic material for a volume with a different slant as a follow-up winner. Also, one book can spawn a number of others on the same overall topic.

The first step—*setting your mind for whatever sustained preparation and effort is required*—is all-important in planning a book proposal. Most book presentations I've reviewed which have failed were shallow, half-baked, and therefore unconvincing. Many amounted to "How about a book on so-and-so?" When I told one budding author that his presentation was inadequate, he didn't think so . . . but the rejecting editor did. Now *you* won't make that mistake.

KEEP THE PROPOSAL COMPACT. DON'T WASTE A WORD!

When you shape up your presentation, review every page before you turn to the next. Cut each word that doesn't move swiftly to your one objective, *getting a publisher contract*. If you clutter your theme with extraneous phrases and sentences, you'll be inviting a lapse of attention from the editorial reader and a lost opportunity.

Concentrate on presenting not what *you* think about the book project (you're prejudiced), but what will convince *the editor* and others at the publishing house to approve a contract. Eliminate everything else, no matter how charming or amusing or impressively "literary" the self-pleasing words may appear to you.

Practically every proposal draft I've seen by a beginning or experienced writer (including all of mine in the early stages) has contained extraneous and therefore disruptive material. Such flab must be chopped ruthlessly. Look for and eliminate any "look how good I am" and "see how beautifully I write" indulgences. Each word must move the editor closer to the conviction that *this book will sell*.

When you think it's impossible to cut more from your proposal, *start cutting more.* My "completed" draft of a presentation for my four-hundred-page *Miracle Gardening Encyclopedia* was twenty pages, much too long. It took weeks, but the final proposal was *four* pages (I'm holding it right now). Those few pages covered the "different" thrust of the book . . . why it would appeal to gardeners more than other volumes available . . . the market scope . . . fifty-chapter listing in detail . . . enumeration of photos, drawings, charts as illustrations. The comprehensive yet compact proposal won quick approval, since the publisher knew exactly what was offered and the profit potential, *proved* by the specific facts included.

ALWAYS START WITH A "GRABBER" TITLE

Many others will tell you, as I've noted, "Don't include a title for your proposed book. Publishers don't like that, they want to create a title themselves. Just present the *subject*." My experience is otherwise. I urge you to devote as much time and creative thought as necessary to come up with an eye-catching title that both appeals and tells what the book is about. It's a bonus for the publisher.

In presenting a title, include a subtitle if necessary (it invariably is). Note these cautions:

- *Beware of being "clever" or "tricky."* When friends react, "Oh, that's cute," try something else. The comment "That's creative" is okay.
- *Be clear and informative.* The best reaction is, "That's a book I want to buy."

A recent best-seller is a good example of a *creative* and informative title (with subtitle), adding up to a "grabber":

EAT TO WIN
  The Sports Nutrition Bible

Here's an example of a title and subtitle that impressed the publisher instantly and went a long way to make the sale:

CONSCIOUS HAPPINESS
How to Get the Most out of Living

I know that the title did its job because when the editorial director read my presentation, he wrote, "Your title hooked me immediately because, like everybody else, I believe in *happiness*. And I'd rather be *conscious* than unconscious. Also, I certainly want to get the most out of living. . . ."

My repeated experience affirms that the right title helps a proposal immeasurably, even if the publisher changes it later. Consider that if you can't come up with a title that conveys the appeal of your proposed book in a few words, then something may be wrong with the book's basic premise, and you'd better remedy that problem first.

STRUCTURE FOR BOOK PRESENTATIONS

Resurrecting the presentation of my twenty-eight nonfiction books to date, I've examined and analyzed them carefully. With some slight variations, all follow the same contract-getting structure presented here for you. This is what has proved successful in getting acceptances:

1. Book title and primary sales point(s). Often noted as possible selling copy for the book jacket, to interest and convince the reader to buy the volume.

2. Market potential. Who will be attracted most to purchase the book . . . size of the targeted audience.

3. Personal background assets. Pertinent biographical facts, experience of author in relation to affirming worth and dependability of the projected book contents.

4. Difference, uniqueness, special values. Why this book can be expected to attract many buyers and help them with its contents, far more than other books in the field.

5. *Chapter contents.* Chapter titles, main points in each chapter.

6. *First chapter of book.* Preferably two or three opening or representative chapters, probably offered as available when publisher is ready to read them after digesting the complete outline and presentation.

7. *Special promotional power.* Quick synopsis of outstanding features to project in all-media publicity and author interviews and public appearances.

8. *Brief covering letter.*

I developed this structure step by step in presenting my first nonfiction book for the general public, *Miracle Gardening*. I prepared the solid sequence painstakingly with one aim in mind—to get enthusiastic acceptance and approval by publishers. The result didn't come out of the blue. It emerged from my special experience in preparing hundreds of productive presentations for advertising agencies.

Proceeding exactingly, examining every detail involved, I studied many of the formats I'd worked on in advertising that had been exceptionally successful in selling campaigns involving millions of dollars. I figured that the formula evolved should work as resultful book presentations, too, as refined and improved with each successive proposal. That structure produced for me. It can for you, if you'll work with it, adapting according to your personal judgment and added creativity.

Essential element: aim to achieve transference. Here I go again, stressing that extremely important point from my Madison Avenue experience: Every word in those advertising presentations was honed to convince the people who had to approve the campaigns. Therefore, realizing that I had to find my way into the minds of the people reading and acting upon my proposals, I achieved the necessary *transference*.

Nothing mystic or mysterious about that. "Transference," according to a dictionary definition, is "the process in and by which an individual's feelings, thoughts, and wishes shift from

one person to another." Stated simply and for practical purposes
here, I evolved the transference in my mind of becoming the ad-
vertiser (client) reading, rather than the agency person writing.

You can accomplish the same by *concentration*, one "secret
of strength" in boosting the mind's powers. As you conceive your
presentation, you can learn to channel your mind's focus into becoming the editor reading, as differentiated from the author
writing. No magic . . . you simply present clearly what the editor
wants and needs to know in order to arrive at the decision favorable to you.

Ready . . . set . . . *concentrate!* Proceed—with this transference in sight—to each of the basic eight stages of the presentation
structure, expanded in detail as follows . . . .

Stage 1: Book Title and
Primary Sales Point(s)

As a proved-successful example for you, I'll use my presentation
for the *Miracle Gardening* book. I tackled this as an aspiring
writer proposing my first nonfiction book. First, over a period of
time, I listed for myself over fifty possible titles for the book.
Checking, analyzing one after another from the publisher's sales-
minded viewpoint, I kept crossing out and reshaping phrases until I arrived at a two-word title. I believed that it packed the power to get exceptional attention and project special, appealing
promise to gardeners.

Then I compressed the primary selling points into just a couple of dozen words after much cutting and refining. I knew I had
to get the message across fast to the editor and publishing staff.
Finally, I was satisfied with my opening page:

Gardening Book Proposal: MIRACLE GARDENING

How to grow bigger, brighter flowers, thicker lawns, and huge
mouth-watering vegetables, using the amazing new scientific
miracle substances and methods.

Plus 1001 Tips for Today's Gardener

By Samm Sinclair Baker

That succinct, irresistible appeal to gardeners, who seek always to grow the best, scored with the editor, who was able to pe-

ruse it in fewer than thirty seconds (I timed my own scanning beforehand). She told me later, "Reading that powerful promise to gardeners, I had to continue instead of stopping at the first page of a proposal as I usually do." (An extra bit of luck—she was a gardener herself.)

It still requires prolonged effort and revising for me to get the proposed title and the primary sales points exactly right in the minimum number of words. You'll find it worthwhile when you get that thrilling call or letter: "We want your book."

Stage 2: Project the Market Potential

My investigations indicate that most book presentations omit this stage. I consider it a valuable element in order to delineate the potential market and emphasize the sales prospects for the book. Always seek and cite dependable facts, not empty superlatives. Keep the data crisp, clear, sound, interesting, never too weighty or lengthy.

In the case of *Miracle Gardening*, I listed figures revealing the impressive growth in the number of gardens and gardeners. I emphasized the accelerating dollar sales of gardening products and supplies. All this grew from extensive research. I quoted authoritative statistics and sources—government agencies, trade journals, newspapers, associations. (The facts have proved out with time.)

The editor asserted, "This material helped me a great deal. I was able to present the sales potential of the book factually to the marketing director and others who have to approve the offer. Instead of saying, 'I think there are a good many people who will want this book,' your data gave me proof of the potential. You saved me a lot of digging in preparing *my* presentation."

Obviously, you improve your chances of gaining a favorable reception, and moving toward acceptance, when you aid editors. Everyone appreciates being saved time and effort.

Stage 3: Highlight Your Personal Background Assets

It's definitely helpful, of course, if you can show a listing of one or more successful published books and any other publications, but it's not essential. I couldn't. So instead of worrying about negatives, I concentrated on the positives.

I stressed my background in gardening, beginning: "At age four, my father gave me some radish seeds. I planted and tended them. I pulled up my first radish, rubbed off the soil, bit it—and it bit me back. I've been bit by the gardening bug ever since. By personal experience, I know how gardeners think, what they want and need. . . ."

I detailed in a few words my work on gardening accounts in advertising, how my copy helped build a mail-order nursery, from little one-inch ads, to become number one with full pages in newspapers: "Sales proved that I know how to write to gardeners." I described briefly my research for the proposed book, contacts with leading agricultural universities, scientists, experts, agricultural agents. All that is available in practically every field.

You don't need special wizardry in your background. If you haven't thorough knowledge of the subject, either through experience or research or other learning, probably you shouldn't be proposing a book. Of course, if you have the know-how or can get it—say so, backed by facts that prove your contention.

How you can become an instant expert is illustrated by a story involving the famous attorney, Clarence Darrow. Late in the day in court, the opposing lawyer brought up a complicated subject. The next morning, Darrow attacked the convoluted topic with high skill. A friend asked, "When did you become such an expert on that matter?" Darrow answered, "Last night in my study, from midnight to dawn."

You can do likewise.

Stage 4: Emphasize
Uniqueness, Superiorities

With *Miracle Gardening*, I foresaw the editor asking, "Why another gardening book?" So I inserted that question in the presentation and answered it by naming specific new, modern gardening aids covered. I listed fresh information and ingenious tips not in any other gardening book. I had studied available books thoroughly, and I made explicit comparisons.

Example: I told about new (at that time) water-soluble plant foods (Stern's Miracle-Gro), as developed in a noted university laboratory by top scientists, naming them. I included photos of tests using radioactive isotopes in a specially prepared liquid solution, checked with a Geiger counter. The fascinating graphics proved that nutrients went from soil to the top of a six-foot-high rosebush in minutes. A limited selection of plant photos, drawings, charts obtained through research sources, plus reproduction permissions, were incorporated in the presentation.

Keep in mind that the editor is human, a reader who will be attracted by eye-catching visual material. So are members of the editorial and marketing committees who must approve the contracts. They're all individuals saying, "Show me." They're impressed when you do.

Don't ignore the competition. In offering *Reading Faces*, coauthored with Dr. Leopold Bellak, I noted three other books published in the past ten years about reading faces. Then I explained exactly how our book would be different and markedly superior. That negated any objections about competitive books which might block a contract.

This presentation included a celebrity's photo with lines on the face, and details about how simply and effectively the Bellak Zone System worked. The editor said later, "I was fascinated, tried the method on my own face in the mirror, then on others. Soon everyone in the office was reading someone else's face, creating an uproar. The clear demonstration in the proposal made this an easy sale."

Stage 5: List Chapter Contents and Brief Descriptions

In each presentation, I include a listing of chapter titles and condensed descriptions of chapter contents under each title. Certainly, that's a great deal of work—*you're actually constructing the framework of the entire book*. That's necessary, I believe, because you're asking a publisher to invest considerable time and money in assessing, editing, and producing your book.

Editors can't recommend a book contract to the editorial and

marketing board without a clear delineation of exactly why the
investment is warranted. Yes, proposed chapter titles and se-
quences are subject to change as you write the book. As an instance, in offering my first coauthored book, *Questions and Answers to Your Skin Problems,* I knew it wasn't enough to list one
chapter heading as "Allergies." Here's how it appeared in the actual proposal:

> *Chapter 4. ALLERGIES AND RELATED PROBLEMS:*
> *Allergy Questionnaire. Allergy to Cosmetics. Food Allergy.*
> *Allergy to Drugs and Chemicals. Sensitivity to Detergents*
> *and Cleansers. Allergy to Insect Bites. Miscellaneous Al-*
> *lergy Questions. Hives. Eczema. Poison Ivy.*

Convey two essential points. Each presentation necessarily
differs, according to the theme and character of the book you're
proposing. Aim to get across these two potent, essential selling
features to the editor and board:

> The scope of the book, and proof that it will provide de-
> tailed information that readers need and want.
>
> The author knows the subject and will cover every essen-
> tial facet authoritatively and dependably.

As noted, some presentations require more detailed chapter
contents than others, as in the case of *Your Key to Creative
Thinking:*

> *CHAPTER 1: HOW THIS BOOK CAN MAKE YOU*
> *MORE CREATIVE*
> *What is Creativity?*
> *Proof That You Can Be More Creative*
> *C.Q. vs I.Q. (Creative Quotient vs. Intelligence Quotient)*
> *Why Your Participation Is the Essential Element*
> *Beware of Negative Thinking*
> *How to Profit in Many Ways*
> *Why the World Needs Creative Thinking and Ideas Now*
> *Rewards Like These Are Great and Personal*
> *Your First Practice Session*

Each chapter was to include "Mental-Exercise Puzzlers."
The proposal provided a few sample puzzlers, of eighty-two
planned for the book, such as this one:

> *ANALYSIS PUZZLER:*
> *THE CASE OF THE MYSTERIOUS LETTER*
> *You, the postmaster in a small town, find an envelope with only three words on the front, this way:*
>
>
>
> WOOD
>
> JOHN
>
> MASS
>
>
>
> *You must figure out the right name, city, state for delivery.*
> *ANSWER: The objective is to analyze clearly why the three words were placed in that particular formation. Why is "JOHN" under "WOOD" and over "MASS"?*
> *Obvious solution:*
>
>
>
> JOHN UNDERWOOD
>
> ANDOVER, MASS.
>
>

When the editor called with a contract offer, he said, "The sample Puzzlers helped sell us the book quickly. I tried them on my family and on people at the publishing house. Their enjoyment clinched it for me, since the rest of the presentation was so solid and promising."

Proof that it pays to be detailed and innovative in your presentation. Just be sure that the attention-getting items make a powerful and pertinent point.

Stage 6: Offer at Least the First Chapter of the Book

You may go on endlessly in your presentation about this "wonderful" book you're *going* to write. However, the proof of the pudding is the offer of at least one chapter. That will demonstrate to the publishers *exactly* what they're expected to buy and present to the public, with a good chance for commercial success.

Particularly when the writer is a beginner, with no published books or other printed material to show, the only validation for the publisher is the manuscript itself—one chapter or more. I've often presented three chapters. Yes, many book contracts have been consummated on the basis of an outstanding idea and presentation alone. You can take your chances accordingly: If the sample chapter is superb, you've advanced your sales potential; if

the writing is lacking, should you be offering it now or improving
it first?

A would-be author complained to me, "That's an awful lot of
work, writing one or more actual chapters—whew!"

I agreed. "By the time I've listed chapter titles and contents
and written several chapters, about one-third of my work on the
whole book is done. But I don't know whether the book will be
worthy until I've put in that much effort. If I'm not sure, I'd feel
dishonest."

The aspiring writer protested, "That much time—it's a *big*
gamble."

"Sure. I look at it this way: If I don't believe in my proposed
book enough to put in that much time and effort, how can I expect
a publisher to have the faith to invest in it?"

Again, *you* must decide how much material you care to
present.

Stage 7: Feature
Special Promotional Power

This can be a valuable asset in proposing your book, if you are
willing to make the extra effort. A number of authors resist publicity—that's okay, too. Based on my background in advertising
and business, I believe that it's up to me, along with the publisher, to promote my book. Therefore, I finish each presentation
with a short synopsis of my own special ability to promote the
proposed book.

I cite unique features in the proposed book which lend themselves to interviews on TV, radio, all media. If you agree, get the
evidence across in a few sentences, indicating that you're eager
to help sell the book after it's published. Be as specific as you can:
Describe what features the book embodies in this area, include a
sample of visual material you can offer, but don't overwhelm the
editor.

You don't have to be an actress or a lecturer. If you have a
background in teaching, that's a natural. Mention any speaking
exposure as a club officer, active PTA member, salesperson. Emphasize ability to inform and instruct people verbally in your book
subject.

Skip this "promotional potential" section if you prefer. I've found it productive to include all the clear-cut pluses the particular book offers. That added projection has definitely helped me get contracts. You'll find the details in Chapter 12 on exactly how to apply promotional and publicity power for more profit from your writing.

Stage 8: Concentrate on Your Covering Letter

Above all, your book presentation must *speak for itself* convincingly. No fancy binders. Just double-spaced loose pages, plus any exhibits, in a simple file folder. If your factual presentation doesn't confirm that your book is worth publishing, then a ton of superlatives in a covering letter, or in your proposal, won't help, and may turn off the editor.

My successful covering letters have been short, right to the point, like this one that worked (reading time under thirty seconds):

> *The proposal herewith for a new nonfiction book*, Reading Faces, *demonstrates its unique content and sales potential: You'll note quickly how you can benefit exceptionally from* reading your own face, *as well as the faces of others, with the simple* Dr. Bellak Zone System. *Thank you for your kind attention and consideration. I trust that I may hear from you soon.*

This is all-important: You must grab and hook the editor's attention right in the first line or two of the covering letter (as I advised for the first paragraph of your presentation). Do that by projecting the most dynamic, attention-getting selling point of the book itself. Study these winning examples:

- *Reading Faces* (from preceding letter): "you can benefit exceptionally from reading your own face"
- *Lifetime Fitness for Women:* "tells every woman, of any age, how to look, feel and function at her peak"
- *The Delicious Quick-Trim Diet:* "lose a pound a day—deliciously!"

The primary purpose of the effective covering letter is two-fold:

1. To introduce yourself by name—no lengthy biographical details, they'll be part of the presentation.
2. To project a dramatic, potent point about the book's theme, which will make reading the proposal irresistible. Toward that result, I urge you to work over your covering letter again and again—revising, tightening, improving—with the same attention and care as creating the presentation and writing the book itself.

SHAPE MAGAZINE AND BOOK PROPOSALS YOUR WAY

The basic structures I've recommended here for magazine and book proposals have worked repeatedly for me and for others I've helped. But understand that *my* way is not the only way. If what I suggest doesn't suit your personal views, then do it *your* way, of course.

As an individual and as a writer, I believe strongly that *if I am not myself, then I am nobody.* You, too, every bit as much as I am, are an individual entitled to your own focus, your own ways, your own sustaining right to be yourself. My proved guidelines, which emerge from both positive and negative experiences as a beginning and then established author, *can* help you immeasurably. How you use and shape what you learn from this book will become as personal as your fingerprints.

In being a writer, the most individual of pursuits, *you must sustain yourself.* If a proposal or presentation is rejected, check it carefully again. If it appears right to you, submit it again. Even a superb presentation may be turned down by a particular editor or publisher for reasons over which you have no control, such as not wanting *any* book on that subject.

Pushing ahead regardless has worked for me, and will for you. Two of my book presentations were rejected sixteen times, accepted on the seventeenth try. In those instances, I went ahead grimly, finishing the total manuscripts while the turndowns were piling up. Both books were extremely successful. The same can be true for you as long as you don't give up.

BE CREATIVE IN YOUR PRESENTATION

As I've touched on earlier, think creatively about including sketches, photos, other illustrations in your proposal pages. A photo, drawing, cartoon, short clipping can be valuable as evidence proving the validity of your ideas. However, use such items sparingly. Be sure that each one makes a specific, impressive *additional* selling point.

Don't let anyone turn you off from being intelligently creative by assaulting you with the hackneyed "It just isn't done." Eye-catchers and clear-cut illustrative proof in proposals have helped me get book contracts in instance after instance, affirming that being original and different *can* work. Many editors have told me that such material, presented succinctly, not overdone, has caught and fixed their attention and interest, helped make the sale.

Computer bonus: If you use a computer (word processor), look into "typesetting" software disks. Such programs combined with a graphics printer enable you to process copy in various types and varying sizes, as though produced by a typesetting shop. You can go from tiny six-point size to letters up to eight inches tall.

On my most recent successful proposal, my sidekick Natalie followed my outline, set pages in differing types and sizes. The impact of type ranging from one-eighth inch to an inch tall was extraordinary. Editors and the publisher who saw and went for the presentation were extremely enthusiastic about the "different," "dramatic," "powerful" impact it made on them.

Consider this as another available selling tool to use now or eventually—to make more money writing.

CHOOSE FROM SINGLE OR MULTIPLE SUBMISSIONS

There is no definitive answer regarding whether you should make single or multiple submissions for magazine and book proposals. You must choose and decide for yourself, in view of these fundamental pros and cons:

Single submissions: You send your proposal to one publisher (magazine or book), then wait for an acceptance or a rejection. If it's turned down, you send the offering to another publisher, and so on. The advantage of submitting to just one publisher at a time is that your chances are greater of getting a reading instead of being turned away unread, since some publishers refuse to even look at a multiple submission. The enormous disadvantage is that it may take weeks or even months for an editor to get to your submissions and convey the decision. A timely topic can die while you wait—total loss for you. The long delays become very trying and destructive for the writer.

Multiple submissions: You make copies of your proposal or presentation and send to as many publishers as you choose. The one generally accepted, fair rule here is that you advise each publisher that you're making a multiple submission. This can impair your chances for consideration since, as I just mentioned, some publishers will not consider multiple submissions. They protest that it's costly in salaries, overhead, expenditure of time and energy to read and consider a proposal. If they accept your proposal and then are told that it's sold already, as one publisher told me, "Everything we've put into considering it, using time to discuss in meetings, is highly expensive and a complete loss."

Increasingly, writers are making multiple submissions, since they can't or won't take the long delays by editors and publishers in coming to a yes or no determination. Now you know what's involved—you'll decide your course with each magazine or other publication proposal or book presentation.

Here's my own judgment as to what's fair to both writers and publishers: On a *magazine* proposal, if I hadn't even had an acknowledgment of receipt after about three weeks, I'd send the same proposal elsewhere (sometimes I'd phone to find out what's happening).

On a *book* presentation, I'd usually wait four weeks before sending to another publisher (again, at times I'd phone to ask what's going on). I've never run into any trouble due to conflicts. Perhaps I've just been lucky. I've always figured I had to take some chances, as in so many facets of living.

FOCUS ON SUBJECT MATTER FOR SUBMISSIONS

A cartoon showed an angry father shouting to his morose, unmoving tot in a playground, *"Play!"*

The point for you is that just as surely as a playground is for playing rather than praying, a manuscript on a specific subject should go to a publisher of magazines or books who favors that topic (along with some others, of course). That fact should be obvious to all, but it isn't. I'm asked frequently by authors (who haven't an agent), "To what publisher should I send my book presentation?"

Just as surely as you wouldn't submit a proposal for an article on infant feeding to *Penthouse*, you shouldn't send a presentation for a book on "The Joys of Sexual Fantasies" to the Baptist Publishing House. The best way to seek the right potential publisher for your particular submission is to look at published books on that subject in bookstores and libraries. The same applies to magazines.

Book and magazine publishers are listed by subject classification in *LMP (Literary Market Place)* and other directories available in libraries and elsewhere. I still recommend that you look over the published books themselves—you'll get the "feel" of which publishers would be most likely to want to consider your book for their lines.

Chapter Eleven

HOW TO MARKET YOUR WRITING TO SELL

You have already absorbed (and undoubtedly are utilizing) the many marketing ways-that-work provided previously in these pages. But I can't overstress the earning fact that even when you write superbly, if your proposals and manuscripts don't reach the *buying* markets for that material, you can't score consistent sales. If off the mark, you'll be doing your talent, creativity, and ability an injustice.

Before I became wiser about marketing facts, I proposed a piece about the involvement of women's clubs in promoting human rights. As the connecting link, findings were based on one person's travels to various clubs across the country. I sent the proposal to the editor of the top travel magazine. Smart? No . . . stupid!

A note from the editor began discouragingly: "Excellent idea, but definitely not for a travel magazine." Of course not. How dumb could I get? The editor continued, "I liked it so much personally that I've sent it on to a friend." The friend, at a leading women's magazine, ordered the article. Saved by a fine editor and a caring individual (who became a good friend). Well, I never said that *luck* doesn't contribute to success. You'll get breaks like that if you keep trying.

The most valuable point here is this: Don't just send your offering to the first market that enters your mind. Study *all* the angles carefully. Ask yourself:

- "Am I approaching the right category?"
- "Am I choosing the best target for my theme?"
- "Am I addressing the correct editor, as checked in directory listings, phone or other inquiries?"

Make sure with each submission, as sure as you possibly can be through checking and double-checking, that you're aiming your offering not only at the right target but at the *center* of that target. That's the surest way to give your writing the best chance to score a sales bull's-eye. Another tip: When choosing the best category and the number one target for your offering, list numbers two and three at the same time. Thus, if you receive a rejection, you'll save time in sending the proposal out again.

AIM YOUR WRITING TO SUIT THE BUYING MARKET

Many selling writers constantly watch for ground swells, for trends in public and therefore publishing interest. Be alert, starting right now, to trends in popular topics in print, items and discussions on TV and radio, and in public forums of all kinds. Keep close track of intensified focus on assorted phases in education, new directions in exercising, styles in fashions, movements in the arts, politics, religion, every aspect of living.

Then seek new twists, fresh creative angles on the subjects of highest public interest, preferably at the beginning of the upsurge. That becomes the "best" market at the moment in many instances. Dig in, offer your original insights developed from research, interviews, the many suggestions in this book.

Don't be concerned about possible accusations from self-elevating nitpickers that you are becoming a "conformist." Be confident about your own inventive viewpoint and abilities and your personal writing approach and follow through.

Of course, you won't *duplicate* what is starting to appear, since that would obviously be rejected. You use your own voice, your active brain, as you wisely plant your seeds in the most fertile media soil *at the most opportune time*. That's when sales grow best.

SEEK AND USE MARKETING
LISTS AND TIPS REGULARLY

Gold mines of information are available to you—all you have to do is to check market lists and marketing tips in publications and directories which you will find are loaded with readily usable current information.

Just a few issues of a writers' magazine reveal detailed lists and current needs of "The Article Market . . . Women's and Service Publications . . . Home and Garden . . . Fillers and Short Humor . . . Syndicates . . . Men's and Adult Magazines . . . Travel," and many more.

If I'd checked such market lists and descriptions regularly, I'd never have offered my book on gardening ideas to the head children's book editor who told me coldly, "You ought to know that we don't publish nonfiction!" (They do now, and she's no longer there.) Avoid such mistakes by scanning monthly listings and annual directories methodically.

As a beginner especially, as well as now, I checked marketing leads in a magazine, sent queries and proposals which led to sales. In one instance, I read an interview with a senior editor at Simon & Schuster, giving his name and what he's looking for in nonfiction. Marketing leads like that are invaluable *when you take advantage of them.*

Whenever writers tell me they don't read the magazines and directories published for them, I ask, "Would you take long auto trips without a road map? You're passing up precious information, inspiration, and learning."

APPROACH SMALLER
MARKETS AS WELL AS
THE BIGGEST

The biggest market isn't necessarily the best market for *you.* Sure, try the leading magazines that pay the largest sums and build greatest prestige when your offerings appear. At the same time, don't overlook publications with smaller circulations where competition is diminished and you have a better chance for acceptance. The important point basically is to *get published*, bringing you income, adding to your record and status as a professional. Each new appearance boosts your reputation.

Writers of plays discovered, when turned away by the big Broadway producers, the value of getting their plays staged "Off Broadway" or "Off Off Broadway" or "Off Off Off Broadway." A number of the budding playwrights worked their way up step by step from "Off Off Off" to the "big time." Follow the lead of many top nonfiction writers who have achieved success by climbing the ladder rung by rung.

As suggested previously, scan the market listings, never skipping the potential market in the *hundreds* of smaller publications that buy short and long pieces. This is one more way to turn your personal special expertise into earning power through writing. If you like to take photos, consider camera publications. Study the magazines for golfers, outdoor sports such as fishing, pet publications, whatever your prime concerns may be. The list is endless: computers, child interests, religious publications, senior activities, hobbies, fitness, education, and so on.

Don't overlook hidden treasure in your own backyard. I suggested to a beginning writer in Larchmont, N.Y. that Anderson's Book Shop, a leading independent local bookstore, might yield a salable story. She dismissed the idea. A few months later, an article on Anderson's appeared in the fine national trade magazine, *Publishers Weekly*—done by a freelance writer living in New Hampshire.

Sectional publications offer local and regional selling opportunities for writers. I teamed up with a psychologist in our town, and we sold a monthly feature to a magazine serving the county. Our columns aimed to help solve personal problems presented in letters by readers—already assigned by most mass-circulation publications. Also, many established authors started, as I did, by selling pieces to local newspapers and then working part- or full-time on the dailies or weeklies.

Trade publications for almost every business under the sun are markets which may not pay as much as general magazines,

but are available for added income. Again, you'll be having your
work published and building up your list of credits.

Specialized publications. You'll find *hundreds* printed in
the writing handbooks and other annual directories. Turning the
pages, you can select from listings which include health, education, agriculture, performing arts, technical and scientific, city
and regional, house magazines, company publications, and more.

Foreign markets offer some possibilities for moneymaking
with original and reprint writing, but are generally overrated in
most writers' minds. For one thing, payment is usually comparatively low, often shockingly so. Discuss the possibilities with
your agent if you have one. Otherwise, my advice is not to go after foreign markets unless they approach you. Use the time more
productively on other more profitable opportunities detailed in
this book.

Markets of all sizes and types are out there. They need loads
of articles week after week, month after month. They're buying
and publishing. Today there are more possibilities enabling you
to write and sell than ever before: Think of the many recent publications in communications, in business and personal computers,
in enlarged recreational concerns, in other markets stemming
from modern interests and advances in everyday living.

You can cash in on the augmented opportunities now. Even
the smallest steps can take you to supreme advances, right up to
the peak of writing accomplishment.

DON'T RESTRICT YOURSELF TO MAJOR BOOK PUBLISHERS

You may not be contemplating the book market yet, but—as a
writer—you undoubtedly will tackle a book sooner or later, as
you should. A book is a major accomplishment for anyone. Even
after thirty books published, I still get weak-kneed with emotion
when I hold the first copy of a new book solidly in my hand. Furthermore, here's an attainable goal for every writer, as you know

from considering the how-tos in this book and others.

Unfortunately, in offering book manuscripts, too many writers overlook the smaller publishers. They may become discouraged after rejections from the biggest and best-known firms. The fact is that *you may be better off* having your book issued by a smaller publisher. Store that in your brain—you may profit in the future.

There are advantages on both sides. I know from personal experience with both types. The major houses publish more books, have longer lists into which your offering might fit. With much greater financing and facilities usually, they can put more money into distributing and promoting your book. Many think there's more prestige in being published by a major firm, even though readers buy title and content, not publishers' names.

On the negative side, your book gets less attention among a lot of other books the big publisher is offering that season—unless yours is considered one of the few top titles in the list. Make no mistake: The prime attention goes to *"lead books";* others may be lost in the shuffle. Large publishers particularly count on best-sellers to "carry" the rest of the line.

The big publisher tells the aspiring author, when advertising and promotion necessarily aren't forthcoming, "Your book will find its way." Sometimes that comes true, mostly it doesn't happen. The problem is primarily the fault of economics, not of the executives. It's a sad fact of marketing life that a publisher, large or small, would soon go broke with a huge promotional budget for every book offered each season.

The list of the smaller publisher encompasses fewer books. Each book tends to receive more attention and push from the firm's executives as well as from your editor. The sales representative can focus more on each book than the merchandiser covering dozens of books on each call. There is less chance that your book will be lost in a mass of titles going through selection, editing, manufacturing, distribution, and promotion in the normal processing at a large publishing house. However, as noted before, the smaller publisher lacks the sheer power of size.

I'm *not* recommending the small book publisher over the huge company, or vice versa. My purpose is to *inform* you about the pluses and minuses of size (true in practically every category of business, education, other areas). The main point for your personal benefit is this: Don't ever overlook the opportunities with smaller publishers in offering books—just as you learned in respect to articles and other writing in the publication field.

MORE FACTS ON MARKETING THROUGH AN AGENT OR NOT

Beginning and selling writers ask me repeatedly, "How can I get an agent?" The query should be instead: "Do I need and deserve an agent?" Volumes have been written on the subject, including some excellent books you'll find in libraries and bookstores. Here, briefly, are my convictions based on my experiences:

You generally waste time, money, and effort in seeking an agent until you are selling enough to justify an agent's attention: An agent gets 10 percent of what you sell, not what you write. An agent may take six months to sell an article for $500, then collects $50 in commission. Often, it takes two years to sell a book for a $3,000 advance, and a $300 commission. That's not nearly enough to pay for the agent's office overhead, salaries, phone calls, mailing costs, etc.

Agents aren't interested in one-shot authors. (There are rare exceptions like a public superstar.) You'd better be able to prove to an agent that you'll be writing and producing steadily year after year.

No agent has a magic wand which will wave and automatically sell an unwanted manuscript. Any writer who blames rejections on not being represented by an agent is indulging in wasteful self-delusion. Write well enough, keep at it, follow through, and *you'll sell*—without or with an agent.

Most successful authors sold without an agent at some time by the do-it-yourself, prove-yourself route. On my own, like others, I sold scores of articles and two books before I sought and teamed with an agent. Many professional writers don't use an agent and don't want one; they believe they do as well or better on their own, especially in selling to magazines.

Don't expect too much from an agent. Many writers look to an agent to sell their stuff, hold their hands, get them publicity, be counselor-lawyer-financier. My excellent longtime agent advises on the direction and quality of my work, selects markets, *gets the best possible prices and contract terms*, then maintains contact with the publisher. He is not my publicist, lawyer, "mother," or shrink. None of that is his business. Marketing and selling my writing are. I've read and heard claims about agents who do everything including washing the author's dirty dishes—I don't believe them.

If you seek an agent, make as certain as you possibly can that your choice is honest and reputable (most are). Realize that the *agent* collects the money from publishers, takes 10 percent (or more, according to prearrangement), gives you the balance. A number of agents belong to the Society of Author's Representatives; you can get from SAR an explanatory leaflet and names of members. Also, you may check The Authors Guild. Both are in the New York Manhattan phone directory (available in libraries).

The SAR leaflet suggests: *"How to Find a Literary Agent:* Agents prefer that authors write a short letter before sending in manuscripts, describing their work and giving a brief resume of their interests. The author should make reference to any of his work which may have been published or performed."

BE ALERT FOR UNCOMMON AND UNIQUE MARKETS

Untypical and new marketing opportunities keep surfacing as public interests vary and expand, and technological and other developments emerge. Some such possibilities include:

Syndication

We're all aware of the "big-name writers" such as Ann Landers, Art Buchwald, and Erma Bombeck. They're syndicated to hundreds of newspapers by huge organizations such as King Features Syndicate and United Feature Syndicate. Most writers think that, aside from the few prominent names, there's little chance to sell a new syndicated feature.

Think again—all these are potentialities: syndication in newspapers, a continuing feature in magazines, a regular series in network and independent TV and radio, cable TV. To offer a feature, prepare a covering letter and presentation, as with a magazine article, add three or more finished samples of the feature you propose. Your idea and writing must be solid to attract readership and audience, whatever the medium.

Without a "big name" or reputation, years ago, I sold features on a variety of subjects to newspapers, magazines, radio. I didn't try TV because I decided to concentrate on print, as most fulfilling for me. However, today I would tackle TV in the same way: letter, presentation, sample scripts—then follow up repeatedly via mail and phone with facts supporting the special appeal of my offerings. (At one time, with a couple of babies adding to cost of living, I had four monthly features under four different bylines in a national magazine.)

As with book publishing, there are many smaller syndicates in all media aside from the giants. Look up the names in marketing lists and directories.

New Markets

Cassettes offer a unique market for nonfiction authors who can provide self-help, how-to writing, information, instruction, inspiration, psychology, health, exercise, diet, many further facets. There are a number of producers of such cassettes; you can obtain their names and addresses by checking comparable cassettes offered in stores and in mail-order ads. Approach the same way as in offerings to other media.

That's a start for you. Keep looking for unusual, unique opportunities and for all new developments that require writing and writers. Speechwriting and ghostwriting are further examples. Practically every phase of living needs writing, offering you further opportunities to make money writing.

MORE SALES POTENTIAL IN NONFICTION THAN IN FICTION

While many writers, primarily the young and beginners, prefer to tackle fiction—for whatever reason—the facts are indisputable that by far the greatest sales opportunities are in *nonfiction*. The following information is drawn from publishing magazines and newsletters and from publishers. I've rounded out the figures and weighted them to be most conservative:

> Number of books published annually: *About 80 to 90 percent of books published (latest figures) are* nonfiction. *This does not include university press publishing, reported as "overwhelmingly nonfiction," or paperbacks, "increasingly nonfiction."*
>
> *Magazine contents listings* reveal that articles and features are so prevalently nonfiction over fiction that percentage dominance figures would be staggering.

The variations of nonfiction listed in the available reports include: anthropology, autobiography, business, criticism, current affairs, economics, history, humor, literary history, mathematics, personal history, philosophy, political science, religion, sciences, sociology. There are many more types of nonfiction books not included in these listings, such as computer field, diet, exercise, fitness, health, and more. All these categories and others provide nonfiction marketing opportunities.

Book publishers have told me that nonfiction is "less risky" from a sales viewpoint. The president of one of the largest publishing companies stated bluntly, "We can usually count on finding enough people interested in the particular nonfiction subject to sell out the first printing, at least, at some profit. With most fiction, it's a gamble."

The point here is *not* to discourage anyone from choosing to write only fiction. That's entirely a matter of personal preference. I've written nonfiction and fiction, including published short stories and two mystery novels. I've found both forms challenging, absorbing, and deeply satisfying. My purpose is to inform you that, factually, nonfiction offers the greater marketing and selling opportunities by far, a better chance to gain dependable and enduring income from writing.

ENJOY EQUAL PRIDE AS A NONFICTION WRITER

The prime purpose of writing *nonfiction* is to inform, instruct, stimulate, inspire, and elevate the reader. In short, nonfiction aims to *communicate*.

Quite the opposite, and just as laudable, writing *fiction* is, at least in part and unavoidably, an *ego trip*. I don't mean that negatively at all. Fiction involves basically the expressing of one's personal talent, thoughts, feelings, attitudes—the inner self of the author.

Both pursuits are admirable and deeply rewarding.

It's unfortunate that a comparatively few fiction writers—a self-proclaimed, self-inflated "literati"—twist that worthy term for their narcissistic self-interest. They believe that they elevate themselves as "better than others" by labeling much nonfiction as "nonbooks." In doing so, they debase themselves, because "better than others" is a bitter acid which corrodes within.

How much better to exert energy to uplift one's own writing through improving quality, creativity, effort, and self-criticism continually, rather than by trying to put down others.

Take merited pride as a writer, nonfiction or fiction, *as long as you write the best that you possibly can.*

CAN YOU SELL TOP-QUALITY NONFICTION WRITING?

Anyone who asserts that nonfiction writing cannot match fiction in quality is either ignorant or purposefully demeaning. The facts

are otherwise, today and always. Editors and publishers are constantly seeking top-quality writing in nonfiction as well as fiction.

As I've emphasized repeatedly, quality writing basically is
writing that *communicates*. Writing has also been called "the expression of human intelligence and imagination" and creativity,
"mind at work discovering reality" and *conveying this reality to
readers*.

The proof that quality nonfiction sells is everywhere on
printed pages. Here's one small sample, a few lines from a very
long article about family doctors in *The New Yorker*, again by
best-selling author John McPhee:

> *These patients live in and near Washburn, Maine, a town
> with some false-front buildings and a street so wide it viv-
> idly recalls the frontier days of the Old East.* . . . *The popu-
> lation is two thousand and, often, not much is stirring but
> Dr. Jones. His office is on the ground floor of what was once
> a clapboard firehouse, its bell tower still standing at one
> corner. Pigeons live upstairs, and even in the walls. They
> make their presence heard. In the examining rooms, they
> provide the white noise. They serve the purpose Muzak
> serves in Scarsdale.*

The better you write nonfiction, the more clearly, simply,
vividly, and evocatively, the more effectively you'll communicate
and sell. There is no ceiling on nonfiction quality.

WHAT SIZE PAYMENT OR ADVANCE TO EXPECT AND ACCEPT?

This is what has worked for me through the years: At the beginning, I never haggled about payment. Whatever the editor offered—$50, $500, $1,000, or more—I said, "Fine, thank you."

Later, as more of my writing was published, I'd ask about
size of payment. At times, I requested more than offered. Never
argued, said politely, "Sorry, $1,000 isn't enough. It's worth
$1,500 to me and, I hope, to you." I'd get the higher fee, or not.

We always stayed friendly, all-important for future relations.

On advance payment for a book, I always figured that I'd earn more than the advance—overconfident, certainly (many books don't even sell enough to cover the advance), but I was lucky. I'd accept what I considered fair, even less if I wanted that publisher—perhaps taking $10,000 instead of a warranted $15,000. If sales earned $15,000 or more in royalty payments, I'd get just as much money.

A very big advantage of a large advance is that the publisher pushes harder to sell enough copies to cover that payment and more. Another plus is that the author has the use of the cash at once for living expenses and investments that gain interest (which the publisher would prefer to earn, of course).

On my first diet book, the hardcover advance was $2,500, the paperback $7,500 (the latter contracted upon hardcover distribution). Some said we coauthors were foolish to accept such small sums, but we were desperate after sixteen rejections. With millions of copies sold to date, size of advance was meaningless.

I don't necessarily advocate your being that moderate. Make up your own mind, as in this example: At a recent Writers' Seminar Lunch, a beginning author said, "A large paperback publisher offered me a $1,000 advance on a proposal for a very short book that I could write quite quickly and easily. I'd be able to incorporate listings and other material I have already. They like the idea but say the market is very limited. Should I take the measly $1,000 or turn it down?"

A well-paid professional snapped, "Reject it! They'll rate you as cheap. And you'll be cutting money offers to others."

I advised, "Try to get more money, of course. Also, study whether it's worth time you might spend on a better-paying project. Consider the value of having a published book in your hand and on your record. Don't tell anyone else the size of the advance. You'll get additional payments if the book sells well."

He accepted the offer and is writing the book happily, knowing he'll be thrilled to see and touch his first published book. What would you do? Sure, seek sound advice, but weigh carefully suggestions that may be good from somebody else's perspective but not from yours. Decide for yourself: only you know what the choices really are and what will satisfy you personally.

TRY TO ARRANGE
A "KILL FEE" IN ADVANCE

Some publications are willing to arrange a total fee for a sizable article—to be paid upon acceptance—and a "kill fee" or, more politely, a "guarantee," to cover the writer's time and expenses in part if the delivered manuscript is deemed unusable. If rejected then, the author gets the kill fee anyhow. *Be sure to arrange a kill fee in advance* if possible, confirmed in writing.

A professional writer told me happily, "I just sold an article to X magazine for $5,000 if final manuscript is satisfactory." I asked, "Since that's a conditional sale, did you arrange a kill fee?" "No, the editor was so enthusiastic, I'm sure it's not necessary."

After weeks of hard work, she delivered the manuscript, which the magazine subsequently turned down. She raged, "They refused to cover my expenses. I'm going to sue!"

"Too bad," I sympathized, "but you were willing to write on speculation, no guarantee. The magazine has no obligation to pay you anything, unfortunately. You'll lose." Her lawyer agreed. Eventually she sold the article elsewhere. If she'd arranged a kill fee, she'd have collected that *plus* the amount from the later sale.

IS IT WORTH PAYING TO
PUBLISH YOUR BOOK?

If your book manuscript is turned down by so many reputable publishers that you despair, and consider paying to have it published, you have two alternatives:

1. Find a printer who publishes books, get a price for *x* number of volumes, secure competitive bids, place the order. You'll have a thousand or more copies in hand (a *wonderful* feeling just to hold your own printed bound book), to give away or sell through stores, mail order, any way you can. You'll pay thousands of dollars, probably worth it if you can afford it readily. Chances are that you won't make back a dime, but you'll gain per-

sonal pleasure unless you count on covering your costs or making
a profit through sales.

A few writers have had their books printed, and built sales to
success, even to the point of having a reputable publisher take
over. A handful of others have taken their published, unsold
books, backed them with their own money and incredible energy
to sell them store to store, putting in month after month of grueling effort. My hat is off to them (I couldn't do it). One or two have
built their books into blockbuster best-sellers. A few have
published their own book, then works of others, and have become
small publishers. Personal rewards can be great. The odds are
overwhelmingly against financial success.

2. Go to a "vanity publisher," who will perform all services,
including a "promise" of distribution and promotion, for thousands of your dollars. How do you proceed with a vanity publisher? *Very, very carefully!* Check every promise made, including
the dots and dashes. How many *bound* books will you get (not
just flat printed sheets)? Do you get all unsold bound copies (if,
indeed, *any* are sold)? Exactly what "promotion" will you get
(usually a token listing among others in a small ad)? *Question every word in the offer.*

Before you sign a contract or pay a dollar, seek advice from
your local librarians, bookstores, any professional you know connected with the writing field. Don't get me wrong—I'm not saying that vanity publishers are crooks, any more than other large
or small businesses which operate for an earned profit, with or
without misleading claims and even outright lies (I learned the inside facts during my decades in advertising agencies).

What would I do? I've always believed in the eventual publication of every book I wrote, surviving as many as sixteen rejections; other best-selling authors have endured dozens of rejections before purchase by a publisher. *But I'm not against paying
for publication:* I've met affluent amateur writers who've gained
joy from their books processed through either a vanity publisher
or a printer. In their position, if I despaired of having my book
published, if it meant enough to me to possess and give bound
copies to others (for whatever reasons), and I could afford it without strain, I'd have a qualified printer publish my book. It would

be easier, and a lot more costly, I think (I don't *know* because I've never paid to have a book published), to use a vanity publisher. Check carefully, and decide for yourself.

The odds are overwhelming that you'd never get back more than a few dollars, if any. If you proceed, do it with your eyes open—no future regrets. You know your own needs, desires, finances. Whatever you decide, with total sincerity *I wish you gratification and good fortune.*

Chapter Twelve

HOW TO PROMOTE YOUR WRITING AT EVERY STAGE

Few writers realize the value of promoting and publicizing their work and themselves in order to help sell more of their writing. When I suggest self-promotion, there's a tendency for many to react negatively: "Nice writers don't do that." If you agree, and are determined to maintain that attitude—okay. My purpose here is to tell you *how* to promote your writing and yourself, to help sell and earn.

I, too, was painfully shy, dreaded even the thought of sticking my neck out to push my writing and myself into the spotlight. So I learned how to use publicity, starting with local outlets, especially the newspaper, to do the promoting for me. What I gained has been enormously effective in selling more writing and more books than would have happened otherwise.

I discovered, right from my start as a writer, that when people know about what you write, and your growth as a writer, *that helps get more writing assignments, more material published, added earnings*. Individuals connected with publishing, and with reading, read about you, hear you, see you, learn about and are reminded of your writing. In subtle, unexpected or direct means, acceptance and demand for your writing mount.

Example: Maxine, a bright, striving writer who'd just had a book published about a specific child-family problem, phoned me and said, "I'm going to be on the *Straight Talk* TV show tomorrow. I'm scared to death. . . ." I watched. When we met again, she sighed, "I was terrible." "I agree—you were uptight, strained, self-conscious, uneasy, *primarily because you hadn't prepared.*"

I explained to her the highlights of the ways-that-work. A few weeks later, she phoned: "I was in L.A. and was interviewed on my book. I'd prepared, as you taught me. The interviewer said, 'You were wonderful!' I was." I'll bet she sold more books the second time around.

The ways-that-work which follow in this section have worked for me from my beginning as a writer and can work for you. Whether or not you apply these recommendations for yourself is totally your decision.

GUIDELINES FOR INTERVIEWS AND PERSONAL APPEARANCES

The sooner you start making public appearances as a writer, wherever that may be—in a hall, on radio, TV, newspaper and magazine interviews—the quicker you'll help boost your writing sales. Even before your offerings are published, there can be more than the usual interest in you, since you are a writer (a writer is one who writes, and keeps writing, whether published yet or not). You're going to be asked to speak out, especially if you make it known, as I recommend, that you are available.

Are you ready to put your best face forward, to project in the way that will sell your writing most effectively? I wasn't at all prepared in my early appearances. I was nervous, unsure, my thoughts organized poorly or not at all. I was unfit, skittish, didn't make an adequate "sell" for myself as a writer, nor for my writing. Are *you* ready to face the public in person?

Believing in the sure payoff from promotion, down to organizing what I would say, I studied how I would get my points across best and not risk a nervous breakdown with each appearance. I approached the problem as I would a self-help article. I analyzed the situation thoroughly, my past poor reactions and lack of productive actions. Based on my conclusions, I created six basic guidelines which have helped me project calmly and with maximum effectiveness (within my personal limits as a writer, as I'm not an actor).

The six basic essential guidelines have supported me through thousands of promotional appearances, talks, and lectures during the years, in just about all media. Using them thereafter, all apprehension vanished. Repeated experiences help, too—tremendously. My best gauge of whether I came across as adequate or better is the fact that I've been asked back with each successive book by most of those who invited me on TV, radio, and interviews for publication. Here are the six supportive guidelines that can aid you as they have me . . .

Guideline 1: Focus Totally on Helping Your Audience

Realize specifically that your own pressing purpose is to *connect*—to reach out and inform, interest, instruct, and help the viewer, listener, reader.

Pleasing an interviewer is desirable, but secondary. Your total concern should be to relate to the public.

Try to forget *yourself* as you concentrate on the person who will benefit from the information you are conveying. That individual is the potential purchaser of the book, magazine, article— whatever you're promoting.

Focus on reaching and aiding him/her/them. With that concentration, you will become oblivious to any possibility of being self-conscious and uneasy. You won't have any pressure within to ask yourself, "How 'm I doing?" *You will succeed in accomplishing what you set out to do.*

Guideline 2: Prepare Thoroughly Before Any Public Appearance

Before any interview or public appearance, whether for a book or article or other subject, consider in detail exactly how you can best reach and impress your audience in order to accomplish your purpose. If you're promoting a book, your goal is to get them to buy your book.

Based on thorough analysis of the book—and of what will convince the audience most effectively—I list the points that I decide must get across. I tape the slip containing those items on the inside of the cover of the open book. I prepare 3" by 5" file cards with more details about each feature I seek to emphasize, tuck them into a jacket pocket where they're handy for quick reference. When talking to a "live" audience, as at a book-and-author luncheon, the cards form the structure for my remarks.

In addition, I attach small tabs to the first page of each chapter, to open for instant reference. For example, in my "interview copy" of *The Complete Scarsdale Medical Diet*, which goes along on all interviews, tabs read: "CHEM" (for Diet Chemistry), "BASIC" (for the primary Scarsdale Diet), "GOUR" (for the Scarsdale Gourmet Diet), and so on. I can turn quickly to note the details of each segment when being questioned.

On one or more 8½" by 11" sheets folded into the copy, I type in more detail the main points to get across, along with actual quotes from the book and the page number. Thus, during an interview, I can open the book instantly to emphasize a particular point: "Here on page 82 is the recipe for Poached Fish Natalie, a favorite on the Scarsdale Gourmet Diet." (When you can hold up and refer to something in the book, that increases the viewer's desire to own the book herself.)

If the book contains illustrative material, such as the bar chart on page 19 showing the protein-fat-carbohydrate content of the diet, I prepare and carry an enlarged chart to show. When promoting the *Reading Faces* book, I took along blowups of photos that appeared in the book of Reagan, the Carters, JFK, and Presley.

In promoting a magazine article, I carry and show the issue, as when *Family Circle* included an eight-page section on *The Delicious Quick-Trim Diet*. That show-and-tell device informs the viewer (if TV), helps the magazine, the article, and spurs the editor to order more writing from you.

When other writers see how I've prepared a book or other subject with tabs, cards, and detailed sheets, the usual reaction is a horrified *"Wow, that's a lot of work!"* Sure it is, but essential and worth it for me. Knowing the subject, and possessing such clear reminders and reference points right at hand, takes off the pressure, leads to confident, smooth, productive presentation.

Guideline 3: Restudy Your Subject Each Time

Before every promotional appearance for a book, as an instance, I reread the book or article (scanning every page, not reading each word). If I have a tape or video cassette of a previous interview on the same subject, I replay it and pay close attention to what went over well and what fizzled. It's essential for me to do that "homework" the evening before any public performance or a day of book touring, as well as early that morning and again just before the interview.

You know from your school days, when you crammed the night before in preparing for a test, that such repeated reviews helped dispel some apprehension and produce better grades. Knowing my stuff and, in effect, rehearsing what I'm going to say in a set talk, or answering the questions of an interviewer, eliminates the pressure of being unprepared and therefore uncertain.

I urge you to try this preparedness system. I was fortified about the worth of this process of tuning up in advance when I came across an ancient proverb: *"He who knows and knows he knows: he is wise—follow him."*

Guideline 4: Talk to Just One Nice Guy

Decide to communicate person-to-person, not with an impersonal mass. That applies to any medium—a "live" audience in a room or auditorium, or on radio or television. Speaking, in effect, with *one* individual, you loosen up and tend to make close contact with the entire audience, even millions, helping every person most. This intimate joining also keeps you from *preaching*, which would invariably turn people off.

I learned this invaluable lesson during my appearance on the Dave Garroway *Today* show on NBC-TV when it was at peak popularity years back. This promotion for my first gardening book was also my first time on TV. I was quaking within as I was seated alongside Garroway at a table, cameras pointing at us, one minute before the live telecast.

Noting my extreme nervousness, Garroway said, "Samm, understand this: I'm a pretty nice guy, and you look like a nice

guy. So forget everybody else. Talk only to me—two nice guys
having a friendly chat. Ignore the clock. When I tap your knee
under the table, you'll know that our time is up." I was amazed
when the tap came—I'd forgotten the audience. Garroway said,
"You were great. Come back at ten for our live broadcast to the
Pacific Coast. We'll cover the same ground all over again."

Delighted by my star performance, I went to my office, also
in Radio City. Dozens of my coworkers in the ad agency stopped
to tell me, "Saw the show, you were terrific—a real pro!" Returning to the studio, I patted myself on the back: "Now you're a real
pro—this time look directly into the camera's eye, right at that
big audience out there. . . ."

The show was on . . . Garroway asked the first question. I
went to answer, stared into the camera lens at 6 million people—
and my stunned mind went blank. I had enough presence to remind myself: *"One nice guy!"* I turned to Garroway, forgot the
masses watching, and sailed through the interview smoothly and
happily.

That tip is priceless, worth the cost of this book alone. When
you're promoting your writing or anything else to an audience,
don't think of the mass. Remind yourself: *"One nice guy!"*

Guideline 5: Speak
Truth Only . . .
No Deception, No Double-Talk

If you don't tell the exact truth as you know it . . . if, instead, you
resort to exaggeration, double-talk, even deception or downright
lies, no wonder you become anxious. Your conscience starts trou-
bling you. Most pressing, *you have to remember those lies* as the
interview progresses so that you won't be caught piling an eva-
sion atop the lie.

Once I said to myself that I wouldn't ever try to cover up
again, or evade the issue, or tell the slightest lie in my public appearances, a tremendous load was lifted from me. Much of my
tension vanished—I was home free. I recommend that course totally to you.

So what do you do when the interviewer, or someone from

the audience, asks you a question or challenges you bluntly—and you don't know the answer? The solution is utterly simple: You simply say frankly and openly *"I don't know."* That eliminates any tension due to knowing that you're faking. Furthermore, people usually realize it when you're putting them on, and they turn against you.

I guarantee to you that "I don't know" is blissfully liberating. The interviewer and audience will appreciate your honesty in saying that you haven't the answer. They'll admire you for your courage in admitting it. *You'll* feel very good, and your message will go across well.

Guideline 6: Accept the Best You Can Do

You've probably heard some of the greatest performers in the world, including Sir Laurence Olivier, whom I heard on TV, say, "I was awful . . . I gave a terrible performance!" If they can miss at one time or another, so can you—especially when you're not experienced at facing the public.

I've had interviews, particularly in my earlier appearances, where I realized afterward that I came across very poorly for one reason or other (sometimes an inept interviewer is at fault). Sure, I've felt rotten about it, and in the beginning, I was miserable, never wanted to face an audience again. When I did go on, I had butterflies because I was afraid that I might flop again.

Then I asked myself a potent question: *"What can they do to me if I bomb?"* Ask yourself that point-blank. As you start to answer, you'll feel a sense of wonderful relief. You'll find yourself realizing that "They won't cut my throat. They won't hang me." Absolutely true. The worst that can happen is that they won't invite you again. (If it's radio or TV, the producer will probably be changed soon anyhow, so no lasting damage done.)

You can live with that. Next time, prepare as recommended. Adhere to these six basic guidelines. Practice and repeated experiences will build your self-confidence, ease, and ability. You'll do better—and you'll be sensationally good eventually!

HOW TO PROMOTE THROUGH YOUR OWN EFFORTS

Recommendations in this section will aid you in getting valuable publicity and promotion for your writing and yourself as a writer *on your own.* Authors like myself who put in the effort know from results that these ways work. Here's a summary:

Get interviews and public mentions by sending brief personal letters and factual usable material to editors, program producers, stars themselves. Always provide a dramatic springboard fact showing exactly how and why the news or your appearance would be good for the newspaper, magazine, or show—interesting and helpful to the particular readership or audience.

Include reprints of reviews, news stories, unusually appealing background facts about yourself and your writing which support your offerings. Include everything eye-catching that would help get attention and approval—but never too much.

Follow through with personal contacts via phone calls, more mailings and information, checkup calls. Try every possible outlet, since getting publicity is *scoring a few hits among many misses.* You must keep trying. I landed an interview on a top network talk show by getting the star's home address (after I couldn't get past his protective staff). I sent him an inscribed copy of my new book, with informative material. He then ordered his staff to contact me, resulting in *two* interviews, which sold loads of books.

Focus on sound content—that's the foundation of publicity and promotion success for all your writing. You must offer valuable, usable, attention-getting information and help—to convince publicity outlets and then make the sale. Innumerable suggestions throughout this book tell you how to find and present such values best, as in all writing.

USE YOUR LETTERHEAD TO PROMOTE YOUR WRITING

As a beginning writer (and now), I included with every submission or related contact some brief, pertinent facts about my personal background, accomplishments, and any available details about use of my writing in print and in other media. I did this to inform and impress the editor that I was a responsible writer (even though my credits weren't substantial).

As my credits mounted, I printed them right on the letterhead. First I lined them up vertically along the left-hand side of the sheet. Later I placed the facts on the back of the letterhead, writing my letters on the blank side (name, address, phone on top as usual). Further down the road, I added my photo (helpful to producers considering me for TV appearances) and highlights of my writing accomplishments.

Favorable feedback was highly encouraging. Many of those receiving the promotional letterhead (with credits on the back) said that they appreciated getting the facts about me at a glance. The device definitely helped to get me more writing assignments, also promotional news stories and interviews in all media.

Other writers asked for permission to copy the idea—certainly I approved, with my blessing. This concept is all yours to adapt to your needs. No authorization needed from me (even if I wanted to, which I don't, there's no way an idea like this could be copyrighted or patented—that would be mean anyhow).

Printing such letterheads is inexpensive. You can type the listings on your typewriter or word processor, have the sheets run off at a copy shop. I use a little copier that serves well for this, also makes reprints of publicity stories, etc., to support my constant promotional efforts.

SAMM SINCLAIR BAKER

1027 CONSTABLE DRIVE SOUTH
MAMARONECK, N.Y. 10543
PHONE (914) 698-5535

BIOGRAPHICAL FACTS:

"America's Leading Self-Help Author" (NY Times)

"King of Self-Help" (NY Sunday News Magazine)

Coauthor #1 & #2 Best-Selling Diet Books Ever.

3 BEST SELLERS

WRITING AIM: To help people live happier, more fulfilling lives.

AUTHOR OF 31 BOOKS IN MANY FIELDS, NONFICTION AND FICTION.

New *WRITING NONFICTION THAT SELLS (Writer's Digest Books/1986)
  *THE COMPLETE SCARSDALE MEDICAL DIET w. Dr. Herman Tarnower (Rawson; Bantam).
  *THE DOCTOR'S QUICK WEIGHT LOSS DIET w. Dr. Stillman (Prentice-Hall; Dell).
     Scarsdale #1, QWL #2 Best-Selling Diet Books Of All Time.
  *THE DOCTOR'S QUICK INCHES-OFF DIET (Prentice-Hall; Dell)—Best Seller.
  *THE DOCTOR'S QUICK TEENAGE DIET (David McKay; Warner) Top Teen Best Seller.
  *THE DOCTOR'S QUICK WEIGHT LOSS DIET COOKBOOK (McKay; Warner).
  *DR. STILLMAN'S 14-DAY SHAPE-UP PROGRAM (Delacorte; Dell) All Big Sellers.
New *EROTIC FOCUS (on Sex) w. Dr. Barbara DeBetz (NAL Hdcover '85; PBack '86).
  *FAMILY TREASURY OF ART w. Natalie Baker, Artist, Wife (Abrams/A&W/Galahad).
  *DELICIOUS QUICK-TRIM DIET w. Sylvia Schur (Villard; Ballantine).
  *READING FACES w. Dr. Leopold Bellak (Holt-Rinehart-Winston; Bantam).
  *CONSCIOUS HAPPINESS, How to Get the Most Out of Living (Grosset; Bantam).
  *THE PERMISSIBLE LIE, The Inside Truth About Advertising (World; Beacon).
  *LIFETIME FITNESS w. Jane Boutelle (Simon & Schuster; Fireside Books).
  *"DOCTOR, MAKE ME BEAUTIFUL!" w. Dr. James W. Smith (McKay; Bantam).
  *STRAIGHT TALK TO PARENTS w. Mary Susan Miller (Stein & Day; Scarborough).
  *YOUR KEY TO CREATIVE THINKING (Harper & Row; Bantam; Reader's Digest).
  *ANSWERS TO YOUR SKIN PROBLEMS w. Drs. Robbins (Harper & Row; Dell).
  *HOW TO PROTECT YOURSELF TODAY w. Police Exec. (Stein & Day; Pocket Books).
  *VIGOR FOR MEN (Macmillan; Warner). *CASEBOOK OF SUCCESSFUL IDEAS (Doubleday).
  *HOW TO BE A SELF-STARTER (Doubleday). *HOW TO BE AN OPTIMIST (Doubleday).
  *MIRACLE GARDENING ENCYCLOPEDIA (Grosset). *MIRACLE GARDENING (Bantam).
  *SAMM BAKER'S CLEAR & SIMPLE GARDENING HANDBOOK (Grosset; Bantam).
  *INDOOR & OUTDOOR GROW-IT BOOK, Children & Adults (Random House).
  *GARDENING DO'S & DON'T'S (Funk & Wagnalls).
  *MYSTERY NOVELS: *ONE TOUCH OF BLOOD. *MURDER (MARTINI), VERY DRY.
New *SUSPENSE NOVELS: *LOVE ME, SHE'S DEAD '86; DEAD-LINE: PARIS/ISRAEL (in work).

  *INNUMERABLE MAGAZINE & NEWSPAPER ARTICLES, STORIES, PRESS, RADIO SYNDICATION.
  *MILLIONS OF FOREIGN LANGUAGE BOOK SALES; Worldwide Articles, TV, Radio, Press.
  *COUNTLESS PERSONAL APPEARANCES: TV, Radio, Lectures, Press Interviews.
  *INSTRUCTOR, LECTURER at Columbia U., New York Univ., U. of Pa., Iona, more.
  *ADVERTISING AGENCIES: former Pres., Vice Pres. *BUSINESS CONSULTANT.
  *NEWSPAPER REPORTER. *CARTOONIST. *GAG WRITER. *EDITOR, College, Schools.
  *TEXTILE LABORER...MILL FOREMAN...RETAIL CLERK...DOOR-TO-DOOR SALESMAN.
  *SCHOOLING: Paterson NJ High School; U of Pa; NYU; Columbia; New School; others.
  *HOMES: Paterson NJ; Allentown, Pa; Grottoes, Va; NYC; Larchmont, Mamaroneck, NY.
  *WIFE: Natalie, Artist, Art Teacher, Classes in Home Studio; Book Coauthor.
  *DAUGHTER: Dr. Wendy Baker Carmer, PhD, Professor, Neuroscience at Einstein.
  *SON: Dr. Jeffrey Baker, PhD Psychology; author of books, articles.

NEVER FORGET YOUR GOAL: SELL YOUR WRITING

To sell your writing, books or articles or other material, you must always keep this target in sharp focus: You're there to sell your book, article, your ideas, your crusade, as you provide the reasons for interested participation by your audience or readership.

You can't just talk or discuss charmingly and pointlessly—in print or radio, TV, other media. Be prepared thoroughly beforehand (as advised earlier in detail). Make the sale by conveying *specific help for the readers or listeners*. Speak up interestingly, proudly, energetically, getting your points across dramatically. Reach out, get excited about the content, convey that electricity—sharing, not overpowering. Remember that a dull piece or interview indicates a dull book or article.

WHAT TO EXPECT FROM THE PUBLISHER

For your long-lasting benefit, you should know the *facts* about what you can expect in promotion from your eventual book publisher, on average. The knowledge imparted here with brutal clarity, based on repeated experience by many, may be unexpected but should not discourage you. Knowing the facts, you'll take steps to get utmost promotion for your book regardless.

Theoretically, the publisher should promote the book forcefully, since he paid for the property, added investment in editing, design, production, follow-through. Most publishers' publicity people, I've found, are capable, energetic. The amount of time and effort they expend is usually limited by how "important" the executives rate the book and the promotability of the book and its author.

Potential best-sellers, most of them preceded by huge advances, are backed by the big advertising, promotion, and publicity budgets. The vast majority of books get little more promotion than a mailing of volumes and a basic news release to a prime pub-

licity list. After that, publishers let a book "find its way," as
they're fond of saying. That's akin to throwing a nonswimmer into a pool and letting him "find his way" or drown.

The author must realize that—however energetically the
publicity people act in launching a book, even a "big" book—in a
few days there's another new book demanding time and attention, then another and another. Each author screams hysterical-
ly, or bleeds silently, wanting more, more, more promotion. But
there isn't enough time or budget to promote each book properly.

Sad but true, most books and authors aren't warranted
newsworthy and salable enough for much publication, TV, and
radio attention. Best-sellers generate a lot of incoming publicity
on their own. So *you must press for all the promotion you can get
from the publisher and exert every possible effort on your own!* If
you just complain to friends, chances are (with exceptions) that
your book will languish and, like an old soldier, slowly fade away.

DON'T COMPLAIN INEFFECTUALLY, OFFER PRACTICAL SUGGESTIONS

There's help for you in my statement which appears in a bright little volume, *The Writer's Quotation Book* (Penguin):

> *My coauthors call me up and get hysterical if the book isn't
> in a big bookstore. I say, "Tough luck." If I have an idea for a
> new display or promotion, I'll send it to the publisher. It's no
> good sitting back and saying the publisher stinks.*

Complaining without presenting impressive specifics turns
publishing people against you (they hear such bitching constantly). I've told coauthors, "Ours isn't the only book in the publisher's list." Typically, a doctor-coauthor phoned me, wailed, "I was
just in a big Fifth Avenue store and they didn't have our book!" I
said, "I'll check and do something about it."

I knew from business experience that it's almost impossible
to get total distribution for anything. In many instances, a huge
food company spends millions of dollars to introduce a new prod-

uct, and you can't find it in supermarkets! In this case, I visited twenty bookstores in the city. I wrote to the publisher's sales director, listed the stores by name, reported that eighteen of the twenty didn't have our book. I followed up with a phone call.

He was upset. "Your findings are shocking. I'll get after our sales reps immediately." I checked the same stores two weeks later: All but two were stocking and selling the title. To get results, back your beefs with facts and positive, practical suggestions—not empty griping and groaning.

GIVE PUBLICITY OUTLETS WHAT READERS LIKE TO READ

To get outlets to use publicity material you send about your writing, the same rule applies that I've emphasized previously for having your writing proposals accepted rather than rejected: *Offer what readers like to read and listeners like to hear.* Furthermore, make your promotional material original, clever, and *usable*. Note this exceptionally successful example:

As producer and a writer of a zany popular network weekly show, *Col. Stoopnagle's Quixie-Doodle Program,* some years back, I decided to promote the show in a different way. I created a press release form headed "Latest Stoopefying Stuff." Each week, we mailed the sheet loaded with gags that "program news" feature writers and broadcasters could use to entertain their readers and listeners. For instance, one week we used these gags on the press release:

- Taped a little transparent bag containing a dozen actual coffee beans on the sheet: "Attached are the makings of a fine cup of coffee, so you can sip while you read this. You know what coffee is—coffee is stuff that's in a cup of."
- "Quixie-Doodle of the Week: Where is it considered a social custom for married women always to wear necklaces? [Answer, printed upside down]: Around the neck."
- "Quixie-Invention of the Week: An alarm clock with only

half a bell, so that when two people are asleep, it wakes only one of them."

More gags were crammed on the weekly sheet. Whatever you may think of them ("Tacky!"), columnists printed and aired them to entertain their audiences. They voted me "Publicist of the Year." I wasn't a publicist but I provided unusual usable material. That's the idea—not to use gags specifically, but to do something creative and different that gets attention and exposure, that puts the spotlight on your writing and you as a writer.

REALIZE PUBLICITY VALUES IN BOOK TITLES

In writing a book, there are many angles to assess, including the publicity values in the title. A short explicit title can be helpful in getting extra attention from editors and publishers when submitted and for exceptional added selling power when promoting the book. Keep this potential in mind.

In interviews, especially on TV and radio, it helps to mention the title as often as possible without dragging it in awkwardly and obtrusively. Obviously, if people hearing you don't remember the title, they won't ask for your book in stores. Think of the title, then, as being so brief and specific that it fits naturally into the interchange with the interviewer. Examples:

> *Reading Faces* provokes an interest at once: "How does one go about *reading faces?*" That's an automatic repeat of the title without dragging it in.
>
> *Erotic Focus* is both the title of the book and the simple self-help technique taught for enhancing sexual pleasure: Naturally . . . "How does the *erotic focus* method work?"
>
> *Delicious Diet:* The key word of the title is emphasized again and again necessarily throughout the interview: "Even though low in calories, the food is *delicious* on this *diet* because . . ."

MULTIPLY THE POWER OF PUBLICITY CLIPPINGS

A writer showed me a superlative newspaper review of his new book. I congratulated him, then added, "Of course, you're making reprints to send to editors and others so they'll be informed and impressed about your writing and you." Surprised, he mumbled, "I never thought of that." If you don't multiply the power of clippings by making and distributing reprints effectively, you'll miss an important plus.

One of the brightest journalists ever, Nancy Q. Keefe, explains the "multiplying" system best in her Gannett interview:

> *His pains won him four inches of space in the* Times, *giving Baker another clipping to reproduce and circulate with his correspondence . . . writing on the back of his résumé or latest clipping, of which he has a great variety.*

> *No sooner had* Publishers Weekly *reviewed his book,* Reading Faces, *than Baker was making copies of his review and sending them off to his publisher with a note full of ideas for using it. . . .*

> *So, he tells the neglected writers [who complain about lack of promotion by publishers], write your own promotion copy, send letters, call people, go on tour. The writers shrink from such behavior, and more of their titles go to remainder shelves at cut prices. Baker's, however, go on selling because he works at it.*

That's your cue: Get promotion and publicity for your writing and multiply the power of every break by *working at it.*

BELIEVE IN YOUR WRITING AND PROMOTE IT

Again, superb journalist Nancy Q. Keefe explains in Gannett newspapers:

A group of suburban writers gather for lunch every six weeks or so or whenever one of them needs a quick fix of gregariousness. Writing, like dying, is undeniably a lonely business, even for those who toil in a crowded newspaper office. . . .

The writers whimper that their publishers will not spend money to promote their book, that the promotion department has written it off even before publication, that the bookstores hide it.

"Tough luck," Baker replies. "What are you doing to promote it yourself?" Horrified, they say it's not the writer's job to peddle books, for heaven's sake. Baker counters, "Who better? If you don't believe in your book, who will?" Believe in the book. That's the key for him.

Worth your thinking about: If you don't believe in your writing and do everything on your own to promote and publicize it, who will?

USE ANYTHING "DIFFERENT" TO INTEREST PEOPLE

Many times you've probably said to someone, "A funny thing happened to me today . . ." You then forget it. Next time, consider whether that incident might have warranted an attempt to publicize your work and you. The following example took only a few minutes to type and send, won space in the popular "Metropolitan Diary" feature in the *New York Times:*

"Here's a city incident that gave me a lift and refutes the contention that New Yorkers are cold," writes Samm Sinclair Baker, who has been described as "America's Leading Self-Help Author."

"I like to wear a rose in my lapel, makes me feel good," he went on. "On book tours across the country and Canada, I have bought roses for up to $1.50 each. In the city last week

for interviews, I stopped at a Park Avenue florist.

"As a pleasant gentleman pinned an exquisite rose in my lapel, I asked, 'How much?' He smiled and said, 'We feel good today—enjoy the rose on the house.' "

A magazine editor phoned me the next day, said she was amused by the report of the incident, and it reminded her of me. The conversation led to an article assignment. Publicity pays— often enough to make the effort worthwhile.

PROS AND CONS OF USING PUBLIC RELATIONS SERVICES

If you want to have your book or other writing promoted professionally, public relations services (listed in the *LMP* directory) are available. For a fee, these companies publicize writer and book in various media, arrange all details of road tours, book the interviews, do everything necessary.

There are pros and cons: Using one of these outfits is costly, up to $1,000 or more per city, depending on size. Honest people in the business will tell you how effective they can be for you personally—or not—depending on promotability of you and your writing. You must check references, size up the service in personal meetings.

I've used such companies on two of my books. An inept publicist was a complete flop, wasting thousands of dollars. The other outfit (Betsy Nolan Group, New York) produced exceptional material and a very successful book tour and promotion. Thus, as with most business dealings, it depends greatly on the people involved, as well as the promotional potential of your writing and you.

My publisher welcomed and approved having the additional services of the fine public relations group (payment by the author automatically increased the total money available). The public relations service worked closely with and under the supervision of the publisher's publicity department.

This promotional tool is worth your consideration if the financing is available. No amount of promotion can sell enough of a book the public doesn't want. Enough force behind the right book and author can boost sales and speed success substantially.

Chapter Thirteen

COAUTHORSHIP: A CHALLENGING WAY TO EXTRA SALES

Having coauthored sixteen books (about half of my published books), all with notable sales, three of them blockbuster bestsellers, I've benefited highly from coauthorship. Here are the guidelines which have worked profitably for me and can do the same for you. But . . . *fair warning:* Agents, editors, and publishers have said that I'm the only multibook coauthor they know who has never quarreled, fought, or broken up with a partner.

If you have or acquire the required temperament—hardworking, reasoned, utterly fair-minded—then coauthorship can be rewarding for you in every way. On the other hand, if you are extremely sensitive, thin-skinned, quick-tempered, very competitive, and unwilling to be concerned about your partner's welfare—even more than your own—I advise you to avoid coauthorship, regardless of how much money you might collect.

The rewards in money earned on books and articles, plus enduring friendships gained, have been incalculable for me. Judge yourself scrupulously, then decide about coauthorship for yourself. In any case, you'll reap invaluable knowledge by reading this chapter thoroughly—to help you make more money writing with a partner or alone.

Note the rejection-acceptance difference that your byline can make when coupled with an accredited expert in the subject: A bright aspiring writer and friend told me that two magazines had rejected her article on prenatal care. She fumed, "It's loaded with good practical advice for expectant mothers, so why won't they buy it?"

I asked, "What's your qualification for dispensing such important health advice?"

"I've just had my third baby, and if that's not sufficient qualification . . ."

When she calmed down, I said, "Wouldn't you be more likely to read an article of prenatal advice bylined by a certified obstetrician *and* a three-time mother?"

The point registered. Her obstetrician agreed to be the coauthor, proposed valuable changes and additions. A magazine paid $1,500 for the piece instead of the $1,000 she'd expected. They split, and she agreed that half of $1,500 is a lot more than zero.

Think about that for your own articles or books on subjects where an expert's name in the byline would impress and attract readers and therefore editors.

TWO WAYS TO ADD THE POWER OF EXPERTS

You can quote one or more experts in a piece bylined by yourself alone and not share the fee, or you can list the authority right in the byline as coauthor, and apportion money received. I've sold many articles and books both ways. I believe that most selling authors, especially those who have achieved professional recognition and stature, prefer to write alone, not sharing either prestige or payment.

The choice depends on this: If I use quotes from more than one expert, I don't offer coauthorship. But if the manuscript is based primarily on material and direct quotes from one authority, I usually favor a coauthorship byline, dividing the fee. Here's what I've found:

1. Sharing authorship splits the responsibility for authenticity of material in the article. I find that when listed as coauthor, the doctor, official, educator—whatever the field—is more concerned, more informative in detail, far more careful in double-checking every statement and bit of information

used. This gives me and editors valuable added assurance that the piece will be sound and helpful for the reader. That's a requisite for my conscience and reputation, also for the publisher.

2. Sharing payment, the expert feels far more involved (remember, I've worked both ways). He's likely to be unsparing in his attention, time, and efforts to make the article or book the best it possibly can be. He's aware that when his name tops the byline, he is held primarily responsible. If merely quoted, he can, and sometimes does, contend that he was misquoted; that occurs in spite of the best intentions of both expert and writer (happily, it has never happened to me).

3. I find it easier to sell writing, on medical subjects particularly, which has an authority's name in the byline coupled with my own. I've encountered many examples like the one in the preceding segment about the writer adding her obstetrician as coauthor. Don't overlook coupling the potent selling power of an authority's name with your own.

YOU DON'T NEED WRITING CREDITS TO REACH AUTHORITIES

You may be holding back because, as a beginner complained typically, "I haven't the professional background or stature or credits as a writer to latch on to a big-shot physician or other expert." Not valid. All you have to do is investigate and list, preferably living near you, some authorities in the field you're researching. Then write or phone for an appointment for an interview if the information is too complex to cover on the telephone.

For a personal interview, you can usually send a short, succinct letter describing the proposed piece, asking for a brief appointment. Then, if no response, follow up with a phone call to arrange a day and time. This method has never failed me, right from my earliest writing days. A brief questionnaire, accompanied by a stamped, self-addressed envelope, and a request to fill in the answers and mail back, sometimes suffices but is usually not enough.

A beginner close to me (our son, Dr. Jeffrey Baker, long before becoming a Ph.D in psychology) was vitally interested in the pros and cons of contact lenses, which he's worn since age fourteen. He researched thoroughly, produced an outline which included many interviews with physicians. An editor liked the presentation, and a book contract followed.

He sought and was granted interviews with many respected doctors and technicians in the field (he preferred this variety approach, rather than coauthorship with one physician). The result was a popular book, *The Truth About Contact Lenses* (Putnam). His procedure in proposing an article would have been the same.

How about you trying this route in writing to sell?

IT'S NOT ESSENTIAL TO FIND THE TOP AUTHORITY

"How can I track down and reach the leading authority in the field?" is a common question from writers. The simple answer is: *You don't have to.* In the first place, it's difficult, usually impossible, to even *name* the "top authority" in any area. More important, few experts are known to the public.

Writers and others often say to me enviously, "You're lucky—your coauthors have always been famous people." That's completely untrue. When I met Dr. Irwin M. Stillman (my coauthor on *The Doctor's Quick Weight Loss Diet*), he was well known only in a small area of Brooklyn where he practiced. Dr. Herman Tarnower (coauthor, *The Complete Scarsdale Medical Diet*) was practically unknown outside of Westchester County, New York. Both became world-famous due to the blockbuster best-sellers.

That spotlights a feature you can stress in approaching authorities regarding coauthorship, if needed—the name in print augments a professional reputation. The result is a payoff for the experts in many ways, including a boost in personal pride. That's a further reason why most of them are not only willing but eager to talk, whether it's just an interview or for coauthorship.

Realize that, as a writer, your efforts *build* reputations for the authorities, as well as for yourself. Be assertive, not shy.

STUDY BUILDING A COAUTHORED ARTICLE INTO A BOOK

After you consult with one or more experts in producing an article or coauthoring a piece, concentrate on the possibilities of building that into a series of manuscripts—possibly a book. That's how you can multiply the earning power of your interviews, perhaps far more than you'd hoped for at the start.

Don't make the mistake of many writers who finish a manuscript, then look afield for "What's the next subject?" Often the potential is right at hand for a series or book on the same topic.

Working on diet material, scoring unexpected successes, spurred me to work up a presentation for a book on the subject. I'd seen and profited from the extraordinary interest in overweight and calories, in the beauty and health aspects of reducing to desired weight and staying trim.

Deciding to make the most of the clear potential, I chose a coauthor, built our dual know-how into one book, adding up to seven books eventually. While multiplying the books, I branched off into a number of high-paying diet articles.

You can do the same: You can coauthor books and articles with one specialist and, at the same time, write and sell manuscripts on many other topics you select, with or without coauthors. However, you must *understand and plan* that expansion—it's not likely to happen spontaneously. Now you realize the possibilities, but you must follow through on your own volition and power.

FOUR GUIDELINES TO SUCCESSFUL COAUTHORSHIP

From what I've learned in writing my sixteen very successful coauthored books and many articles to date, I've analyzed for you the steps and missteps involved in coauthorship. Understand this well: Coauthorship is not all "blue heaven," no more than marriage is. In a way, a coauthorship is akin to marriage in the close relationship and contact between two people—with many of the same benefits and pitfalls.

It will pay you, in considering coauthorship, to give thorough attention to these four basic guidelines:

1. Select a salesmaking subject that excites you.
2. Choose a coauthor with exacting care.
3. Establish equal partnership, equal respect.
4. As the writer, be the leader-manager.

If you can live with and fulfill these four guidelines totally, as explained in detail in the following pages, then you're ready to proceed further with coauthorship of a book (an article is much less demanding, of course).

Guideline 1: SELECT A SALESMAKING SUBJECT THAT EXCITES YOU EXCEPTIONALLY

Let's face it: Coauthorship brings difficulties that don't exist when you're writing your own thing alone. Among other obvious problems that arise in any partnership, unless you handle them with alert care, you must deal with another personality who has specific ways, ideas, even prejudices that you may not approve of and will upset you repeatedly.

Therefore, be sure that the subject is of very special interest to you, involves you thoroughly, aims at a goal you want to achieve very much. If the topic doesn't grip you strongly, if you choose it just for money, approach with caution. Troubles tend to mount, and you might lack the will to exert the special effort required to overcome them.

The desirable choice is a subject with potential best-seller power, that appeals outstandingly to you personally and to your coauthor. Nobody can guarantee that you'll score best-seller sales, but at least the realistic potential should exist. Too few writers assess marketing prospects prudently—do you? Certainly that approach is highly "commercial," but it doesn't negate *quality*. Being commercial means to me selling loads of books, thus helping many more people, as well as earning more.

How to judge a book's sales potential? You must weigh the facts objectively, unmoved by someone else's honest but perhaps overblown enthusiasm. For example, a doctor phoned me from across the country: "Let's do a book together on my specialty, orthodontics. There are tens of millions of people concerned, most will buy. We'll have a good book, and a record-breaking best-seller."

I replied bluntly, "There are two kinds of good books: a good book that sells big, and a good book that sells a few thousand." The marketing fact is that not enough people buy books on orthodontics, because the basic advice is: *See an orthodontist*. Most of the afflicted don't need or want a book to tell them that. Nor will I (or you) write a book that raises false hopes. Helpful information, yes. Empty promises, no.

Writing an honestly enlightening book is worthwhile, but you should know and accept the limited possibilities. A close friend coauthored a fine book on cancer with a leading specialist (*Toward the Conquest of Cancer*, by Stuart D. Cowan and Edward J. Beattie, Jr., M.D.—Crown). As I had predicted, and they accepted, it sold some ten thousand copies, was not a best seller. They were gratified that it helped even a limited number of people, as attested by laudatory reviews and letters. However, the writer, a former marketing executive, knew in advance that prevention, necessarily the major thrust of the excellent advice provided, usually doesn't sell big.

You decide whether or not to proceed without great expectations—as long as you know ahead, and don't gripe afterward.

Guideline 2: *CHOOSE A COAUTHOR WITH EXACTING CARE*

Above all, learn from my unbreakable rule: The prospective coauthor/expert and I must "fall in like" (very close to love) quickly, or it's off. I make that clear immediately. I've been fortunate that all my coauthors have become close friends, enhancing our lives in every way. That's a tremendous plus of coauthorship.

However, *fair warning:* Agents, editors, and publishers have told me that I'm the only writer they know who has achieved such close, enduring relationships with all his coauthors. A key is that you must subjugate yourself, taking second place in jacket and catalog listings and in the public eye.

Most writers can't accommodate themselves to playing second fiddle—they crack sooner or later, and friction ensues. I used to question why stars of movies and theater demand top billing in the titles, ads, on marquees. Now I know—usually the public doesn't even *see* second billing. Even today, after more than 10 million copies sold, with my name as large as Dr. Tarnower's on the jacket, people say, "I have the Scarsdale Diet book, but I never realized that you wrote it." If you can't take that kind of thing, better avoid coauthorship.

When I first approached Dr. Tarnower, I said, "We must like each other very much right away, or it's no go." After some talk, he smiled, "Okay, Samm, I like you very much, how do you feel about me?" I responded, "It's mutual." We shook hands, began a wonderful relationship that never sagged.

In reverse: A publisher offered me a sizable contract to coauthor a book on back problems with a famed orthopedic surgeon he'd lined up. I met the expert at his hospital office, arose abruptly after ten minutes, and said, "I'll think about it, get back to you." I called the publisher: "No deal." "Why turn down a 'big advance'?" "He's a huge egotist, I don't like him—period. No amount of money could compensate for the aggravation and distress."

Realize again that coauthorship is something like marriage. You'll invite serious trouble if you and your coauthor don't mesh strongly.

Another tip: Weigh the promotional abilities, or lack, of your proposed coauthor. The talent and eagerness to speak up on TV, radio, lectures, newspaper and magazine interviews, are extremely valuable in selling books. That influences publishers considerably in seeking a contract.

Guideline 3: *ESTABLISH EQUAL PARTNERSHIP, EQUAL RESPECT*

It's essential to agree on equal status immediately. Case history: Dr. Stillman and I clicked as individuals, had reached the same conclusions about reducing most effectively. Then he said, "I suppose the doctor gets 90 percent of profits, and the writer 10 percent." I responded flatly, "I'm sure from my business experience that the only sound working partnership is equal partnership. My terms are always fifty-fifty on earnings . . . byline is expert '*and*' writer, never 'with' or 'as told to' . . . both names same size type. If you don't agree, no deal."

We parted amicably. He phoned two days later, "Okay, fifty-fifty." We remained close through five triumphant books until his death at age eighty. Since then I've been offered as much as 90 percent of the earnings to coauthor a book, but have always refused since I'm convinced that a lopsided partnership spells t-r-o-u-b-l-e.

Furthermore, if you're concerned about the expert putting in less time and work on the book, forget the whole deal. At a conference, a panel of five coauthors said that the writer's attitude must be, as one asserted angrily, "Get every dime possible for yourself—screw the expert or he'll screw you." What a way to live and work!

I protested, "My attitude, as in our marriage of over thirty years, is to care more about the well-being of the other person than about myself. That has resulted in sixteen successful coauthorships." I was booed by panelists and many of the audience of writers. I guarantee to you that a greedy, self-centered attitude toward a coauthor breeds failure. But if you're willing to work harder and care "beyond the call of duty" for your partner, coauthorship offers exceptional opportunities for attainment and fulfillment.

Guideline 4: *YOU, THE WRITER, ARE THE LEADER-MANAGER*

Note this key point that I've never seen or heard emphasized by any published coauthor. I recommend this with the utmost gravity and necessity: The writer must be the leader and manager on the coauthored project, or it may never be finished and published successfully.

Why must the writer manage the undertaking? Very simply and clearly: because writing a book or article is *your* business, not the line of work of the "expert." That's why I tell each prospective coauthor at once, "You're the professional expert, I'm the professional writer, so I'll be the leader-director-manager. I'll take charge. I'll make the endeavor go and grow."

Every coauthor has expressed great relief that I'd take the responsibility. Typical reaction, "Marvelous. I wouldn't know how to begin. I'm a doctor, not a writer or publisher." Dr. Tarnower was enthusiastic, then curious. He held up the mimeographed diet sheet he had been giving patients for nineteen years, asked, "How do you make a book out of one page?"

"I see at least three books," I explained. "We start by improving the diet. We add several alternate diet variations, a lifetime program. We tell how and why the diet works. We answer most-asked diet questions, include calorie tables, and so on." I handed him copies of the planning notes I'd made before the meeting, and a chapter outline as a starting point. He said, "That's wonderful, you run the show. You're the writer, I'm the doctor."

You must maintain the lines clearly. With the ground rules set, Dr. Tarnower was a superb coauthor, a hard worker, great contributor. But one day he handed me the first chapter which he had approved enthusiastically a month before, said shyly, "Over the weekend I rewrote the first chapter—see what you think." I read it, frowned, spoke softly, "This is awful, Hi—amateur. It's look-how-good-I-am writing—instead of pointing every word to tell the dieter precisely what she wants and needs to know to lose weight—"

He interrupted, "You're right. Throw it out, do whatever you want. As you said—I'm the doctor, you're the writer. You're in charge." A wise, fair, intelligent man. We enjoyed a most gratifying relationship as coauthors and friends until his tragic death.

Another necessary warning: It's risky to coauthor a book with another *writer*. It's not impossible, as proved by some effective such coauthorships, but obvious arguments arise as one writer's choices of expression differ from the other's. A married couple I know, both fine selling writers, quarreled constantly, almost divorced in coauthoring a book. On the other hand, my wife and I happily coauthored *Family Treasury of Art* (Abrams)—lines clear: Natalie the artist, teacher, art historian, I the writer.

You must be ready to take the lead, to keep the manuscript moving, to run the show pleasantly, not bossily—or perhaps coauthorship is not a desirable course for you. Some coauthors can write well . . . it's a pleasure and timesaver then to use as much of what they write as fits.

COAUTHORSHIP WITH A CELEBRITY OR STAR: DIFFERENT GROUND RULES

What happens if you suggest coauthorship to an important celebrity or star on an idea you have and get a favorable response? Or what should you do if a personage or publisher offers you a coauthorship opportunity? That becomes a different ball game. I recommend that you consider carefully. The ground rules differ from those described previously.

I've refused such offers after detailed consideration. In most instances, the star wanted more than 50 percent; I understood and appreciated why. I decided not to accept less than half for the extensive time and work I judged would be involved.

Furthermore, while I enjoy the company of most celebrities and stars, I find them generally more volatile in attitudes and dealings. I wouldn't subject myself to coping with excessive egos in so intimate a relationship. Of course, stars aren't all superegos, but it's tough for anyone to handle the constant praise and adulation equably. Also, a star would be less likely to accept my essential leader-manager role. Invariably they refuse equal billing to the writer in the jacket byline, usually insist on smaller type for the writer's name, and "as told to" or "with" rather than the "and" I demand.

You can't blame the celebrity. The prime success of such a book is due to the star's huge notoriety and following as a starting point. The main reason for the writer to become coauthor is to cash in on that, rather than personal enthusiasm about a subject.

So you may be surprised that *I recommend such coauthorship* if you're a beginning writer. You decide if it's worth the money, the extra care, patience, and self-control in dealing with an unpredictable celebrity. If I were not well recognized and established, *I'd probably jump at such a chance to earn and get published,* to accept a lesser percentage, and endure the probable ups and downs. Again, you must weigh the potential gains against the probable tribulations.

SIGN A FAIR COAUTHORSHIP AGREEMENT

It's necessary to sign a fair coauthorship agreement, just for basic understanding, so far as I'm concerned. Other writers use attorneys, who usually insist on detailed contracts. I'm probably too trusting. Here's the one-page agreement used, with slight variations, on my first fifteen coauthored books:

> *As mutually agreed, Samm Sinclair Baker and (coauthor) will together write a book tentatively titled (working title). Both parties agree that they will share equally in the proceeds, including subsidiary and any other rights. Publishers will be instructed to make payments promptly, half to Baker and half to (coauthor).*
>
> *Signed..................   Date...................*

Since my coauthor and I both used my agent on these books, the sheet stated that "all proceeds from the book will go directly to (agent), who will pay promptly to the coauthors, half to each, after deducting agency commission. Total agency commission on North American sales is 10 percent; on English collections 15 percent; and in translation and in all foreign countries where a co-agent is engaged, the commission is 20 percent."

My sixteenth coauthored book involved two agents (mine

and my coauthor's) and a longer but still simple agreement. Added details included: exact wording of byline; allocation of expenses; distribution of rights in case of death; similar sharing on any succeeding books related to this one, but not on other writing; no assignment of rights to anyone else.

If you use attorneys, the contracts will become lengthier, as perhaps they should. The single sheet served me well because I trusted my coauthor right from the start, and vice versa. I've had no problems, but others tell me I've been lucky. You do as you see fit, as always in respect to my suggestions.

HOW TO WORK WITH COAUTHORS MOST EFFECTIVELY

"Just how do you work with a coauthor?" That question is asked of me over and over again—not only by writers but also by people in all walks of life who are deeply curious. I think that, in a way, they're asking, "How do you handle a *marriage* or any intimate relationship best?" (So now I'm a marriage counselor, too!)

The answer about how to work with a coauthor most effectively (and perhaps the same in a marriage) is definitely this: *There is no one way.* A differing procedure evolves in each instance. How you proceed and continue triumphantly is shaped by the ability, character, personality, and working time and habits of the coauthor. As a writer, you *know* how you work, but now you must learn the ways of your coauthor and respect them.

"How do you work with a coauthor?" In every case, first I dig in to amass all the basic facts and information I need to get started. I obtain some of that essential material from my coauthor. To that I add data, usually the major part, from my own digging and research. Often I get considerable help from files on that subject which I've filled over the years.

Next I shape up a structure which becomes the presentation for an article or book. The latter takes longer and becomes more detailed and complex, of course. I give the proposal or presentation to my coauthor for study and suggestions. Finally, we both are satisfied. Then offer it to publishers.

A difficult, grueling period may follow, as publishers usually take a long time to make a buying decision. If there are rejections and resubmissions, the pressure worsens as the coauthor—who is generally ignorant about publishing procedures—becomes increasingly worried, fretful, desperate. The writer must become a psychologist, soothing and reassuring the patient. It ain't easy, friend. But it's interesting.

One doctor-coauthor, aged seventy, kept wailing as rejections stretched over two years before the sale, "Samm, I'll probably die before the book is published!" It worked out okay—the book became a historic best-seller as he lived another ten years. You must be prepared mentally to handle such problems, as in a marriage.

Once a book presentation is accepted and contracted (champagne time—ecstasy!), I write and move the manuscript along. I do more investigating on my own, ask my coauthor-expert for specific material I need. After this necessary groundwork, I write a chapter. I give or send it to the expert, who approves, corrects, adds, deletes, as needed. I proceed with the next chapter, and the next. The process repeats.

Some coauthors supply their own written material, often excellent, which I use or rewrite, as little or as much as necessary. Both expert and writer review the total manuscript separately, repeatedly, until both are satisfied. Final manuscript goes to the publisher—via agent if there is one, otherwise directly from writer to editor.

The following four case histories delineate differing patterns of coauthorship procedure in my personal experience. There are as many variations as there are coauthorships, as I've noted. However, these should give you a very sound understanding of what you face. You'll learn some reliable and successful ways in which you can proceed, if you decide to undertake a coauthorship.

HOW TO GET STARTED ON A COAUTHORSHIP

My first coauthorship was with a husband-wife pair of dermatologists (true to my guidelines, half the proceeds went to me as writer). We were friends, and at dinner one night, the man said, "We collect gardening books for our country home. Recently we bought yours—*Samm Baker's Clear and Simple Gardening Handbook.* It's the first book we've seen that really makes gardening clear and simple—and exceptionally enjoyable."

The doctor went on, "We think you can do the same about skin problems—make them clear, simple, very helpful to every reader. That ready aid from a book is needed desperately by millions of people of all ages. How about coauthoring such a book with us?"

We talked, agreed. Getting started was difficult. I couldn't dredge needed material from them, although they were very eager. As amateurs about writing, they didn't know how to provide substance from out of the blue. I was just feeling my way in my initial coauthoring venture. I didn't realize that I, as writer, had to take the lead, to specify in precise detail *exactly what was needed.* We floundered, time passed. . . .

Finally, the woman doctor said, "Look, here's how we work in our practice: Our patients ask questions, and we answer them, providing guidance. Also, we ask questions, and the patient answers, so that we can advise intelligently."

Solution: We agreed on a question-and-answer format, but I realized that they couldn't move on their own. I, as writer, had to provide the questions. After many weeks of researching skin problems myself, in medical libraries and elsewhere, I came up with twelve hundred questions. I arranged them on sheets in categories: proper care of varying types of skin, allergies, teenage skin problems, the aging skin—twenty-three chapter divisions total.

To make it utterly simple for my coauthors, I typed four questions per page, leaving large spaces under each, so the doctors could write in the answers, which they did sketchily. While the brief answers were inadequate, I found that I could fill in from there, because I had to in order to make the coauthorship work. I was learning the hard way that, as the *writer*, the prime responsibility and effort were mine. I accepted that. We were rolling.

In a number of nighttime meetings, I asked more questions, made detailed notes, taped their comments (usually I don't tape

since I work best from my own notes). At last I was able to create
a presentation after many back-and-forth interchanges with the
pair, by mail and in conferences.

The proposal was approved by the first publisher who saw it.
A contract followed. From the accumulated material, I wrote
chapter after chapter of manuscript, which shuttled to and fro.
The resultant thick manuscript was approved enthusiastically by
the editorial board. Hardcover, paperback, magazine excerpts,
articles—all proliferated profitably.

My first coauthorship added up to an immense amount of
work extending over more than a year. It was worthwhile for me.
Ask yourself, "Do *I* want to take on such a burden?" Only you can
answer.

ANALYZING, CLARIFYING, ADDING MATERIAL TO MAKE A COAUTHORSHIP WORK

As I've noted before, I had been collecting and filing notes and
facts for a diet book for ten years while I sought the right doctor
as coauthor. Fortunately, I found Dr. Irwin M. Stillman, whose
ideas and goals meshed with mine. In my first visit to his home
for a conference, he gave me two good-sized grocery cartons
filled with bits of paper bearing notations, short and long memos
he'd jotted to himself, some tattered and crammed steno pads,
medical articles, and reprints.

Utterly confused, I dug into the bewildering assortment in
my home office. Accepting the responsibility as writer, I finally
created order from the bits and pieces, much like fitting together
odd-shaped segments in a mammoth, complicated jigsaw puzzle.
I added a great deal of diet material of my own. I took notes during
several meetings with Dr. Stillman, along with many phone
conversations in which he answered loads of questions I'd listed
beforehand.

I mailed chapters to him, which he'd work over and return.
Sometimes he wouldn't alter a word. Other times he'd suggest
changes and corrections. Early on, I created a presentation,

which he approved. During the course of sixteen publisher rejections ("Diet books aren't selling"), we finished the total manuscript. The seventeenth publisher said, "Okay." The book grew
into a blockbuster best-seller.

As a result, we coauthored four more highly successful diet
books and loads of articles, including the first Computer Diet (a
hit!). After the initial book, I knew so much about diet, and about
his ideas and reactions, that we'd meet a couple of times for planning (he had moved far away to Florida). Then I'd write successive chapters which he returned with a very few but essential
comments.

This became an easy coauthorship after the first enormous
load of work I had to provide as the writer—or we'd have failed.
Be prepared to put in whatever work is required—to earn the rewards. Our historic coauthorship success was based on a mutual-
ly respecting, loving relationship. He had a delightful sense of humor. In a TV interview, he said, grinning from ear to ear, "Samm
Baker is the *second* greatest diet authority in the world." Then he
added, "Guess who's the *first* greatest!"

EVOLVING A WORK PATTERN TO FIT A TOO-BUSY EXPERT

How do coauthorships develop? As explained, my first venture
arose spontaneously during dinner talk. Another stemmed from
a chance meeting, was spurred by my having coauthored other
books (that could help you eventually). I met a high police official
when he came for his daughter, a student in Natalie's home studio
art classes.

He said straight out, "I stay trim on your *Doctor's Quick
Weight Loss Diet*. How about writing a book with me on people
protecting themselves, their families, homes, businesses?
There's tremendous public interest and a crying need for a good
how-to book."

We liked each other very much, quickly agreed on working
together and on the book's essentials. He sent me scads of printed
material which I combined with a good deal of data I had located
on my own. I worked up a presentation, as usual, which he

okayed. Publisher interest developed quickly on this hot topic, and a contract followed.

An unsettled working arrangement evolved because my co-author was an extremely busy official. With crises arising constantly, his hours on and off duty were very irregular. Personal contact was difficult. At my request, he supplied a mass of mimeographed and printed material available for police and public use, articles culled from police and other trade publications, other miscellaneous data.

As usual, I wrote chapters which he reviewed and returned by mail or messenger, often via his daughter attending the art classes. I gained information on the phone whenever he could squeeze in the time. Finally, we had a solid, informative book which sold well.

Important lesson: *You find ways that work, no matter what obstacles are in the way!*

HOW AN EXPERT-RESEARCHER EXPEDITES COAUTHORSHIP

Note this clear-cut example of how an expert who is also an experienced researcher can ease and speed a coauthorship. My wife, Natalie, art expert, is also an intelligent researcher. We had often discussed the need for an illustrated book which would open the door for *everybody, all ages,* not just devotees, to the wonderful world of art, for their extra enjoyment and personal enrichment throughout life.

We decided to team up to accomplish this—she the art expert, I the writer. We recognized a need for clear, compelling, informative writing, avoiding the usual pompous, convoluted wordage about art. We determined to interest readers by bringing fifty of the greatest artists of the Western world and their art *alive* in pictures and words.

Our presentation for *Family Treasury of Art* covered three artists (Michelangelo, Rembrandt, Picasso) and their work, four pages each of reproductions, half in full color, an intimate three-hundred-word narrative about the artist and his approach, and detailed captions for each picture. The world's leading art book publisher, Harry N. Abrams, Inc., went for it.

This efficient procedure evolved: Natalie, the artist-historian-researcher, provided about a dozen typed pages of background and explanation about each artist and her selections from their masterpieces. As the writer, I compressed this indispensable material into three hundred words of stimulating, informative narrative about each master, using some of her splendid writing with little or no change. Captions under the reproductions were supplied by the art expert, condensed by the writer.

The resulting magnificent 9½" by 12½" volume contained 330 superb reproductions and enlightening, uplifting reading. *Family Treasury of Art* became a popular seller in its category, as well as a labor of love for both coauthors.

Treasured tip for you: Consider enlisting a coauthor who relieves you of an enormous amount of work by contributing the essential research material in clear, ready-to-use form.

P.S. She doesn't have to be your wife (or husband).

SUMMARY OF ESSENTIALS FOR SUCCESSFUL COAUTHORSHIP

Summing up, in addition to all the preceding recommendations, here are basic considerations for you:

- Fundamentally, you must evolve the one best way to work in each individual coauthorship.
- You must examine beforehand and then determine how to handle the inevitable problems which arise from carrying through any long-range project with another person.
- You must apply great and constant patience, understanding, and "give"—as in all close partnerships.
- You must understand that it may take a year or more to coauthor a book, primarily due to back-and-forth delays involved. There are exceptions. Because of pressure from our

publishers for speed, we finished *The Complete Scarsdale Medical Diet* in only three months. When we toasted our superb aides and ourselves, Dr. Tarnower said, "Samm, it's lucky that you and I are workaholics!" (I don't consider myself a "workaholic," since I *enjoy* writing so much.)

I've gained tremendous gratification (and earnings) from coauthorships. You can, too, if you follow the basic guidelines provided here. At the very least, now you have a realistic idea of what's involved. Obstacles *can be overcome* by coauthors through mutual goodwill, caring, and intelligent, always patient stewardship and hard work by the writer especially. However, if you're not a *cooperator*, avoid coauthorship.

Chapter Fourteen

HOW TO SELL THROUGH SELF-HELP WRITING

"Self-help writing means helping readers to help themselves. It does not mean self-indulgence for the author. Every word must be focused and set down to be productive for the *reader;* otherwise, it doesn't belong in the manuscript. Of course, self-help writers should draw upon what they have learned from personal experience which can be of *proved* valuable aid to readers."

That quote is from a talk I delivered to a large audience at the Iona College Writers Conference fifteen years ago. That approach is the basis of my success in self-help, how-to writing (the two terms are synonymous). *It can be for you.* It will pay you to keep it in the forefront of your procedure in any self-help writing you may do.

CONSIDER SELF-HELP WRITING FOR EXTRA INCOME

Whatever your prime interest as a nonfiction writer—fact, reporting, biography, history, science, psychology, philosophy, on and on—you can earn sizable *extra* income through self-help, how-to writing. Consider the unique opportunities: Whatever your life-style, *you have some special personal knowledge* from living experience that you can impart to others for their profit and your own.

In addition to being challenging and absorbing for the writer who seeks to make contact with others through this form of communication—the written word—the learning conveyed is exceptionally valuable for the reader. That's why so much how-to is published—past, present, and certainly in the future. *This is self-education in action through writing and reading. Note this unique advantage for you. . . .*

You can continue with whatever writing you find most gratifying (including fiction, if that self-expression pleases you most) and still take time out to gain more income through self-help pieces, which might then grow into a best-selling book. From the beginning, whatever I was writing (mystery stories and two suspense novels), I interspersed with self-help pieces, which helped pay the rent. In my case, I earned considerably more money than through writing fiction.

In the end, I found myself concentrating primarily on self-help writing. You may or may not wish to follow a similar pattern—that's totally a personal choice. I'm not trying to push you in any particular direction. I'm simply presenting the features so you can think about them. I welcome your competition because at this point in my career, I care more about *your* welfare than mine. I wrote this book primarily to help *you*.

GAIN SPECIAL PERSONAL REWARDS FROM SELF-HELP WRITING

Here are some of the built-in personal rewards available through self-help writing:

- You can collect added income, inherent in writing to sell.
- This focused factual and inspirational creative thinking and targeted follow-through can improve *all your writing*.
- You learn to *dig deeply*, to concentrate, to cut away excesses, to probe and provide solutions to readers' problems clearly and productively.

■ You *pinpoint your thinking and writing* in driving to a specific goal, to help readers help themselves—and only by succeeding in aiding others in this attainment do you make your work acceptable.

■ You add to your own *happiness in living* by helping others and increasing their gratification and profit from what they've learned due to your efforts. I've received masses of letters from readers expressing gratitude for their gains from my self-help writing. That outstrips the rewards I've obtained from all my other nonfiction and fiction output. You can obtain similar deep personal fulfillment.

If you'd welcome the multiple rewards in self-help, how-to writing, here's exactly how to go about it. . . .

SELECT A SUBJECT
THAT FITS
YOUR PERSONAL
KNOW-HOW

From your background, interests, and work to date, you have gained specific, practical knowledge from daily living and observation that you can impart to others. For example . . .

■ If you keep house and raise a family, you can convey how-tos about solving everyday problems with spouse, children, neighbors, tradespeople, others. You can sell cooking shortcuts, recipe tips, housecleaning energy-savers, sharing chores with neighbors, finding time for self-improvement, painting rooms. You possess hundreds of personal knowhows from which you can profit by putting them down on paper effectively.

■ If you're an office or plant worker, executive, are employed or are an employer in a store, business, factory, government work, in education, other profession, hospital and health activities, social service, sports, and on and on, you can pass along insights that will help others help themselves.

Does this pay off? No question about it. You are far more of a multifaceted person than you have realized. You can draw from your work, for example, as I did from my experience in advertising, which led to trade paper articles, consumer publications, a book—*Casebook of Successful Ideas*, then *The Permissible Lie: The Inside Truth About Advertising*. I funneled my gardening interests into articles, newspaper syndication, a radio syndicated series, five books. Lifelong daily exercising and sports participation led to many articles, two fitness books.

What's your personal passion? Lazing around? How about an article on how to get the greatest enjoyment from leisure time . . . or from being a goof-off? You get the idea: *Begin your self-help writing from your own living experiences to sell how-to pieces that benefit readers.*

FOCUS ON PEOPLE'S PRIME INTERESTS AND NEEDS

Editors and publishers of magazines, books, newspapers, and other media know that their success depends on informing people about their prime personal interests, needs, desires. So pinpoint your self-help writing on what your potential readers care about most. Looking into the possibilities is easy and enlivening.

To start: You're an alert, interested individual or you wouldn't care at all about writing. Go to newsstands and libraries and note what editors buy from writers to serve their particular readership. Heighten your awareness of what people are talking and griping about, what solutions they're seeking in various areas, what's in the news in print, on TV and radio. Then write to answer readers' needs, on the subjects that excite and stimulate you most.

List publications that publish material in those areas, as noted on contents pages. You'll be encouraged to see the abundance of self-help features included. You probably have a better chance of selling to smaller magazines at the start than to mass-circulation nationals (see market listings in directories). Local newspapers and newspaper magazines provide another market possibility. Then write a query letter or submit the completed manuscript.

Here, culled from current magazines, are a few examples of topics to consider for your own how-to writing endeavors: "Controlling Colds for Greater Comfort" . . . "Better-Sleeping Tips" . . . "Handling Interfaith Marriage Problems" . . . "How to Be a Smart Investor" . . . "Creating Personal Sewing Income." Tackle subjects that interest readers and you, and you're on your way.

Just glancing through the Sunday newspaper, I jotted these and dozens more potential writing/selling starters, all grist for your self-help writing mill: "New Findings in Stress Factors" . . . "Installing Your Own Phone Extensions" . . . "New Police Booklet Offers Self-Protection Tips" . . . "Making Dollars with a Home Computer."

Go!

"WHERE'S THE BEEF?"— THE HOW-TO?

A doctor in one of my classes who sought a side career in writing showed me an article he'd done about backaches. He complained, "It contains very authoritative how-to self-help information, so I can't understand why four magazines have rejected it."

Scanning the piece, I spotted the vital flaw immediately. "You tried to write a how-to self-help article," I explained, "but you've covered only *what is*, the types and symptoms of backaches. You haven't told readers exactly what they can do to help themselves—you omitted the *how-to*."

He nodded energetically. "You're absolutely right. I was blind, then blamed editors rather than myself."

How often have you made that error? It's worth rechecking your rejected articles now—and those you plan to write—for similar mistakes. Revise, and avoid such oversights in the future. Chances are that you'll make the sale, as the doctor did eventually followed by many article sales since.

RESEARCH POPULAR SUBJECTS: GATHER INFORMATION . . . CONSULT EXPERTS

First settle on a subject of high interest to editors and readers, either from your own experience and knowledge or from the wide range of other possibilities. Then start gathering the facts you need to write the piece so that it will be salable. Search for fresh angles, new developments, recent advances. Sources of information include libraries, schools, government offices.

Just a rehash of familiar, frequently discussed facts will be rejected—and predictably so. You make the sale by digging *deeper*, putting in more innovative thought, devoting *extra* time and effort. How? The following details expand on a piece I've touched on before.

Let's review step by step what happens with a comprehensive article about a health problem (as if this is your chosen topic). As a beginning writer, I zoomed in on the subject of headaches because I'd been afflicted with them since early childhood. I assessed the facts I'd accumulated, sent a query letter to a top women's magazine. Back came a rejection slip on which was scribbled: "Good stuff, but done too often before." I tried another editor; flat turndown.

Searching further, I spotted a newspaper item about a "Headache Clinic" at a hospital thirty miles away, headed by a leading specialist. Flash: *Consult an expert.* I was surprised at how easy it was. I phoned the clinic, said I was preparing a magazine article, was granted an appointment. I brought a list of questions, had an hour with the authority, left loaded with self-help possibilities. I sent an expanded, detailed query to another magazine, *stressing up-to-the-minute findings by the prestigious doctor.* The editor phoned: "We'll buy six thousand words."

Expert cooperation is forthcoming readily because of the publicity value for the specialist and his work. Make calls, knock on doors. For an article on how to make more money, interview local bankers, stockbrokers, accountants; if one turns you down, try another. Dental self-care: Call on your dentist. Shopping tips:

Food store manager. Don't hesitate to contact specialists in any field. You'll be performing a valuable service by bringing their work to the attention of a wider public. At the same time, you serve readers and yourself.

Again, don't be discouraged because a subject has been covered often before. Originality consists of writing about it in a fresher, more informative, more beneficial, and therefore "new" way. Investigate enough, and you'll find the needed salesmaking leads. It's rewarding and exciting, like tracking down ingenious clues for a detective story.

BECOME AN "EXPERT" THROUGH SELF-HELP WRITING

When your article on a topic appears in print, people consider you an expert (well, aren't you now?). They offer opinions, ask your advice. There's special enjoyment in digging for information and obscure angles and imparting your findings to others. It's stimulating, makes life more fun. And comical things happen along the way. . . .

For one thing, you become deeply involved with each subject—to whatever extent you wish. You'll probably become a believer, like me. In writing *"Doctor, Make Me Beautiful!"* about cosmetic surgery, I had an eyelid-lift and a chin-lift. . . .

Working on the book *Lifetime Fitness*, I practiced the "natural-actions" indefatigably, built muscles on muscles. . . . (still do).

When I started writing *The Doctor's Quick Weight Loss Diet*, I weighed a too-heavy 160 pounds, reduced to 150. Working on *The Complete Scarsdale Medical Diet*, I dropped to 145 pounds. Upon completing *The Delicious Quick-Trim Diet*, I went down to 140 pounds. Wife Natalie warned, "No more diet books, or you'll *vanish!*"

What happened to you, or someone you know, that you can convert to help readers help themselves and thus add income through self-help writing? Have you a neighbor who has lost a lot of weight, overcome a tough marital problem, conquered a serious illness? Have you found an exceptional activity that improves your life-style, can aid others? Are you an extraordinary cook and baker whose recipes will please readers? Apply the how-to writing lessons you learn through this book, then pass on your valuable personal expertise, and profit accordingly.

A MAMMOTH PAYING MARKET FOR HOW-TO

If you have any doubt about the size of the market for self-help, how-to writing, here's further proof: Scanning my newspaper this morning (during the writing of this book), I noted a full-page ad of Barnes & Noble bookstores offering over one hundred how-to books by mail. Here's a selected Baker's dozen, indicating the large variety of subjects published:

- How to Cut Heating and Cooling Costs
- How to Build a Deck
- How to Get Rid of Wrinkles in 5 to 10 Minutes a Day
- How to Invest in Gold
- How to Raise Money for Anything
- How to Redo Your Kitchen Cabinets and Counter Tops
- How to Stay Ahead Financially
- Energy-Wise Cooking
- Growing Food and Flowers
- Cashing in at the Checkout
- Easy Ways to Save Energy in Your Home
- Build Your Own Furniture
- A Consumer's Guide to Contact Lenses

That's only about one-tenth of the listing of self-help books offered. Don't get me wrong—these are not best-sellers, nor were they expected to be. The publisher bought them from writers, invested money, aiming for profit for the business and the author. No question that here's a sizable publishing opportunity. So . . . what's your particular expertise or interest?

Get going—and don't forget the three keys to make money writing: 1. Subject . . . 2. "Grabber" . . . 3. Rewrite.

Chapter Fifteen

MORE ENDURING WAYS-THAT-WORK FOR YOUR SUCCESSFUL WRITING FUTURE

A courageous woman I've never met wrote me: "The sudden death of my husband plunged me into the depths of depression and despair, to the long, slow climb back up the mountain. . . . I made it back up again, taking courses at adult schools and a local college. I fell into creative writing courses—what the hell, I used to write many years ago before I went into secretarial work, so why not give it a fling?

"Fling, nothing! It propelled me into a whole new bright beautiful world. I've labored hard and long, studied furiously, involved myself with writers' workshops and conferences and doggedly kept on writing. This past March I sold my first piece! For about a year I've been writing a book, acquired an agent (through a friend), who is this week—maybe today!—hand-carrying my first eight chapters plus summary to a publisher.

"And now I'm 'bursting with ecstasy' (page 19 quote from your *Conscious Happiness* book). The worst that can happen? Rejection. But I won't quit. . . . My life is richly rewarding, active, and varied with my rebirth and I greet each new day with expectation. . . . I'm never bored!"

Reading that letter has been a repeated uplift for me—and now for you.

CASH IN ON PREVIOUSLY REJECTED WRITING

Realize that some or much of your previously rejected writing can become money in the bank after you apply what you learn here. After you absorb the recommendations and put them into practice, you'll take this step: You'll gather all of your rejections for reexamination as soon as you can. You'll reread the opening paragraphs carefully, objectively, with fresh, clear-sighted analysis—as if through the editor's eyes.

Then ask yourself: Do the opening lines reach out and grip readers, pulling them into the rest of the article? If not, rewrite until you have created a solid reader grabber, even if it means rewriting dozens of times. You'll have a far better chance of having your writing read and bought.

ABSOLUTE ESSENTIAL: YOU MUST PUT IN THE WORK

Added to everything you learn here and elsewhere about how to make money writing, remember that you must put in the work, the time and effort. Without that blood, sweat, and even tears, you may never hear the cheers on your success.

Some years ago, I was interviewing writers for soap opera scripts. It often happened that I'd ask the would-be writer, "What soaps do you watch?" "Oh, I don't watch them, I despise them." "Hmmm . . . let's see your sample scripts." "Well, I've never written any, but I know I can." Such individuals wanted the chance, but wouldn't put in the work to prove they deserved it. Unless you make a total effort in your writing, you won't reach your money-making goal.

HOW TO MAKE TIME FOR YOUR WRITING

During my years as an overburdened advertising executive, I wrote nine published books, nonfiction and fiction, articles, stories, scripts. An ad magazine report on me and others who wrote books pulled a storm of irate letters like this: "I'm too busy in my work—where do these bums find the time to write books?"

My published suggestion to them, and now to you: "During a typical week, jot down at day's end how many hours you spent watching TV, listening to the radio, doing hobby work, attending social affairs, lunch and dinner dates, movies, playing golf or tennis, bowling, sailing, skiing, dreaming in an easy chair, gazing out of a bus or train window, etc., etc.

"It's no more commendable to write a book than to engage in any other pursuit. I write to make money and for personal gratification. Make your own choice, but stop griping that 'I'd write books and articles too if I had the time.' Time exists—it's up to you how you use it.

"Incidentally, I wrote most of those nine books and the rest while commuting on trains forty minutes each weekday, on airplanes, weekends, vacations. No, I don't spend every out-of-office minute writing. Sometimes I even look at girls."

Even swamped by business or raising a family, if you care enough, by scheduling your time you *can* make money writing.

KEEP PROBING THE POTENTIALS IN COMPUTERS AND ONCOMING "MIRACLES"

Writers generally love computers or hate them, few in-betweens—except me and perhaps you. I tried for weeks to master a word processor, gave up. My fault—I didn't want to apply the required effort and time (don't let anyone fool you that learning is a snap). Fortunately, Natalie was intrigued, studied, conquered—so now I type a page, scrawl all over the sheet, and she types it into her word processor, returns a clean printout swiftly.

Here's how it cuts my writing time and work more than 50 percent: I used to type a chapter (or write by hand if no machine were near), scrawl extensive revisions between lines, in margins, on the backs of pages. Then I'd retype, scribble revisions, retype. Weeks later, I'd start the next chapter. Now I write a chapter, hand it to Natalie, *roll right on to my next chapter immediately*. She returns a corrected printout shortly . . . I make more revisions, hand to her . . . get clean copy back . . .again and again until completion.

If I didn't have this help, *I'd force myself to learn and use a word processor*. You do it your way, but please don't let blind prejudice impede your progress as a writer. If, like some others, you still insist, "My battered twenty-year-old portable (or even a chewed pencil stub) is just right for me," fine. Just keep writing . . . and keep probing the role of computers and other developments as *new opportunities* rather than threats.

Back in 1970, farsighted editor Arthur M. Hettich of *Family Circle* asked me to create a "Dr. Stillman Computer Diet." Working with computer scientists, it took as long as in writing a book to complete the project. We had to feed the mass of questions, answers, and advice into the computers before a personal diet based on the individual's needs and preferences could be spewed out swiftly by the machines.

A reader filled out a form in the issue, tore out and mailed it with a modest fee, received a custom-tailored reducing diet based on her data. Because of tremendous reader demand and satisfaction, the feature appeared repeatedly. Sizable extra earnings for the coauthors. *Family Circle* donated profits "to aid research in the field of nutrition and weight problems." A good deal for everyone, but it wouldn't have been practicable or possible without computers.

New developments with potential added earnings are proliferating regularly: Computer software programs and cassettes on a multitude of self-help, information subjects . . . "talking books" . . . how-to, exercise, dance instruction, many other videocassettes . . . on and on. It pays to be alert and open-minded about new developments that can spark increased possibilities.

Example: We never visualized it when we wrote the book. Now Bantam has brought out a computer software package of *The Complete Scarsdale Medical Diet*—unexpected extra earnings! You can cash in too on computer and other new developments on self-help and other writing.

FOSTER ETHICS IN YOUR WRITING . . . AND BENEFIT IN EVERY WAY

To you, and every member of the writing "family," I have repeatedly stressed *ethics* in writing—honesty of expression, and presenting sound information, always striving to help others in some way through every word. Let's each of us, as writers, regard "ethics" not just as a word or dictionary phrase—"a system of moral principles"—but in the full meaning expressed by Albert Schweitzer:

> *Ethics means concern not only with our own welfare but with that of others, and with that of human society as a whole . . . improvement of the condition of the world.*

Please consider this as you write: Much gain can be made if each of us writes and acts for the *benefit* of the whole public—all those actual and potential readers out there. As writers, communicators, and creative individuals, we can uniquely serve many. The benefits are enormous: As you strive to aid others through your writing, you help yourself get the most from every writing day—and every day.

SHOULD YOU PAY TO HAVE YOUR WORK CRITICIZED?

Some years back, as a beginning writer earning twenty dollars a week as an office workhorse, I cut down on meals and other essentials in order to send money to an advertised "literary agent/critic" for mail comments on my manuscripts. The "criticisms" were trite, run-of-the-mill, valueless—except that I did write fresh material to send. Other writers have reported similar experiences: "Money thrown away."

Recently, I met a young writer who said he'd worked for one of the many such literary agent/critics who thrive on reading fees. He explained, "My conscience made me quit after a few months. With an overflow of work and limited time per manuscript, we provided shoddy, stereotyped comments at best, ending with encouragement, usually unjustified, to induce more manuscripts and fees from even impossible writers."

That's typical of other reports. A known writer told me, with shame, "For the money, I let my name be used in ads for an outfit, without criticizing a single manuscript myself." There may be exceptions—I'm no expert here. From long business experience, I don't see how such setups, or huge mail-order "writing schools," can provide expert, thought-out, valuable individual critiques without charging extremely high fees or else losing their shirts.

If you're impressed by the offering literature of a mail writing course, if the fees strike you as reasonable and you can well afford them, this could be worthwhile for you. At the least, the regular mailings would present a continuing writing challenge (but if you pay and drop out, you lose everything). When I was a kid in grade school, I wanted to be a cartoonist as well as a writer. I saved up my after-hours earnings, paid for a mail cartooning correspondence course. It taught me tricks that serve me even now (and I sold a number of cartoons).

In my early days, and now, I've gained a great deal from instruction and helpful criticism from attending writing courses, especially workshops, lectures, conferences, local adult education classes. But a note of caution: In a store, I signed and handed a copy of the Scarsdale Diet book to a lovely, heavy lady who pressed it to her bosom and implored desperately, "Mr. Baker, is this book guaranteed to reduce me?" I said, "Not holding the book. You have to go on the diet." Similarly, taking a course won't bring you success; *writing without letup will.*

I made my way by offering ideas and writing to publications year after year, amassing rejections until I clicked. I still get rejections, so I try somebody else and write more-more-more. I don't know any other way.

"HOW LONG DOES IT TAKE TO BECOME A SUCCESSFUL WRITER?"

This is my personal "guarantee" to you, in answer to that often asked question: *You're going to become a successful nonfiction*

writer *IF YOU WRITE ENOUGH.* "Write enough" is the key. I've never known anyone who wrote enough who wasn't published finally. "How much is enough?" When you make the first sale. And another. And another. You're on your way from then on!

If you're really a *writer*, you'll accept and win with that guarantee. You keep writing, you keep learning. After years of rejections, when my first book was published at last, I crowed to myself, "I've made it—I'm a bona fide author!" But, vaguely dissatisfied, I decided, "With my next book, I'll have made it." After my second book, I predicted, "Well, my *seventh* book will be the benchmark." Still that doubt . . .

Now, finishing this, my thirtieth book, I proceed with my established attitude: "I'll just try to make each volume better. . . ."

At times when a work has been rejected repeatedly, and I've just about given up hope of acceptance, this reminder has always helped me: I enjoyed the challenge and the writing, learned from the experience; next time I'll score. I've found that such optimism, as the epigram affirms, is "a kind of heart stimulant." Keep writing, it has paid for me and hundreds of thousands of writers; it certainly can for you.

How long does it take? Ah, the exciting, stimulating, fulfilling objective of being a writer—an inner secret that we all share: Someday I'll write it right.

Welcome friend.

WANT FAME AND CELEBRITY AS A WRITER?

A bonus from writing for many is the opportunity to gain a certain fame, to be some kind of celebrity. Sure, that happens . . . people read your stuff, note your name, recognize you from TV and lecture appearances. If that gives you a thrill, *enjoy.* Just keep in mind that fame has been called accurately "an empty bubble," "a fickle food upon a shifting plate."

Grandson Michael at ten told me flat out, "The kids in class say you're famous, my teacher says you're famous, but to me—*you're not famous.*"

I agreed, "To me I'm not famous either."

The phone rang; lovely Fran, local librarian, advised that a
book had arrived, added, "I read your profile in the *New York
Times* yesterday—your name is becoming a household word."

I responded, "The only household word I can think of is
Drano."

Fame is fun but fleeting as it flushes down the drain. Writing, the word, is solid and permanent.

SEEK AND SAVOR
THE SPECIAL JOYS
AS A WRITER

As we conclude . . . welcome, friend, to all the special joys available in the wonderful world of writing. Now, more than ten years
after I quit decades of work in businesses, I still bless each morning: "This is *my* day, to use as I like best, working at writing."
And then *doing the writing*. No noisy meetings. No pressurized
conferences. No back-stabbing conflicts with my coworkers.

Sure, a writer's life involves tensions, anxieties, downs as
well as ups. But you enjoy *exceptionally* delightful surprises and
amusing occurrences. Such as: Right now I'm best known for my
Scarsdale Diet blockbuster, but as guest speaker at a women's
club, I talked about my subsequent book, *Reading Faces*. I explained in detail with photo blowups exactly how to read faces.
When I finished, a pretty lady ran up and said breathlessly, "I'm
so pleased to meet you, Mr. Baker. I read *Reading Faces*—and
lost twenty pounds!"

We writers gain deeper revelations, as John Cheever noted
in an interview: ***"The need to write comes from the need to
make sense of one's life and discover one's usefulness."*** Undoubtedly you, like me, feel best when exploring innate and developed mental capacities to the greatest extent in writing. We
share with John F. Kennedy the supreme rewards he sought from
"the full use of my powers in the pursuit of excellence."

MAKE EACH WRITING PROJECT A NEW BEGINNING . . .

One of the greatest compensations from writing is that each oncoming project brings the thrilling challenge and uplift of a new beginning, as for me in writing this book. I've tried to pack every page with practical, valuable aid for you. While I've enjoyed writing fiction in my published stories and mystery novels, my greatest personal gratification by far has come enduringly from my *nonfiction.*

That is based on the flow of mail and comments attesting that I've been able to help millions of people gain greater happiness and more fulfilling lives through informative, uplifting, instructional self-help and other nonfiction. I wish you, too, that special expanding reward, along with your own increasing pleasure and profit in every way from your writing . . . and selling.

Never forget our good fortune, as writers, that each act of creative expression is increasingly an adventure, a stimulating beginning. The son of the immortal artist Renoir wrote about his father:

> *On the morning of his death at age 78, he painted some flowers—and he said, "I think I'm beginning to understand something about it." Then he put down his brush and added, "Today, I learned something."*

I hope you have, too.

Samm Sinclair Baker

Index

Other Books of Interest

Computer Books

The Complete Guide to Writing Software User Manuals, by Brad M. McGehee (paper) $14.95

The Photographer's Computer Handbook, by B. Nadine Orabona (paper) $14.95

General Writing Books

Beginning Writer's Answer Book, edited by Polking and Bloss $14.95

Getting the Words Right: How to Revise, Edit and Rewrite, by Theodore A. Rees Cheney $13.95

How to Become a Bestselling Author, by Stan Corwin $14.95

How to Get Started in Writing, by Peggy Teeters $10.95

How to Write a Book Proposal, by Michael Larsen $9.95

How to Write While You Sleep, by Elizabeth Ross $12.95

If I Can Write, You Can Write, by Charlie Shedd $12.95

International Writers' & Artists' Yearbook (paper) $12.95

Law & the Writer, edited by Polking & Meranus (paper) $10.95

Knowing Where to Look: The Ultimate Guide to Research, by Lois Horowitz $16.95

Make Every Word Count, by Gary Provost (paper) $7.95

Pinckert's Practical Grammar, by Robert C. Pinckert $12.95

Teach Yourself to Write, by Evelyn Stenbock (paper) $9.95

The 29 Most Common Writing Mistakes & How to Avoid Them, by Judy Delton $9.95

Writer's Block & How to Use It, by Victoria Nelson $12.95

Writer's Encyclopedia, edited by Kirk Polking $19.95

Writer's Guide to Research, by Lois Horowitz $9.95

Writer's Market, edited by Paula Deimling $19.95

Writer's Resource Guide, edited by Bernadine Clark $16.95

Writing for the Joy of It, by Leonard Knott $11.95

Writing From the Inside Out, by Charlotte Edwards (paper) $9.95

Magazine/News Writing

Basic Magazine Writing, by Barbara Kevles $15.95

Complete Guide to Writing Nonfiction, by the American Society of Journalists & Authors $24.95

How to Write & Sell the 8 Easiest Article Types, by Helene Schellenberg Barnhart $14.95

Newsthinking: The Secret of Great Newswriting, by Bob Baker $11.95

Write On Target, by Connie Emerson $12.95

Writing Nonfiction that Sells, by Samm Sinclair Baker $14.95

Fiction Writing

Creating Short Fiction, by Damon Knight (paper) $8.95

Fiction Is Folks: How to Create Unforgettable Characters, by Robert Newton Peck $11.95

Fiction Writer's Help Book, by Maxine Rock $12.95

Fiction Writer's Market, edited by Jean Fredette $18.95

Handbook of Short Story Writing, by Dickson and Smythe (paper) $7.95

How to Write Best-Selling Fiction, by Dean R. Koontz $13.95

How to Write & Sell Your First Novel, by Oscar Collier with Frances Spatz Leighton $14.95

How to Write Short Stories that Sell, by Louise Boggess (paper) $7.95

One Way to Write Your Novel, by Dick Perry (paper) $6.95

Storycrafting, by Paul Darcy Boles $14.95

Writing Romance Fiction—For Love And Money, by Helene Schellenberg Barnhart $14.95

Writing the Novel: From Plot to Print, by Lawrence Block (paper) $8.95

Special Interest Writing Books

The Children's Picture Book: How to Write It, How to Sell It, by Ellen E. M. Roberts $17.95

Complete Book of Scriptwriting, by J. Michael Straczynski $14.95

The Craft of Comedy Writing, by Sol Saks $14.95

The Craft of Lyric Writing, by Sheila Davis $17.95

Guide to Greeting Card Writing, edited by Larry Sandman (paper) $7.95

How to Make Money Writing Fillers, by Connie Emerson (paper) $8.95

How to Write a Cookbook and Get It Published, by Sara Pitzer $15.95

How to Write a Play, by Raymond Hull $13.95

How to Write and Sell Your Personal Experiences, by Lois Duncan $10.95

How to Write and Sell (Your Sense of) Humor, by Gene Perret $12.95

How to Write "How-To" Books and Articles, by Raymond Hull (paper) $8.95

How to Write the Story of Your Life, by Frank P. Thomas $12.95

Mystery Writer's Handbook, by The Mystery Writers of America (paper) $8.95

On Being a Poet, by Judson Jerome $14.95

The Poet's Handbook, by Judson Jerome (paper) $8.95

Poet's Market, by Judson Jerome $16.95

Programmer's Market, edited by Brad McGehee (paper) $16.95

Sell Copy, by Webster Kuswa $11.95

Successful Outdoor Writing, by Jack Samson $11.95

Travel Writer's Handbook, by Louise Zobel (paper) $9.95

TV Scriptwriter's Handbook, by Alfred Brenner (paper) $9.95

Writing After 50, by Leonard L. Knott $12.95

Writing and Selling Science Fiction, by Science Fiction Writers of America (paper) $7.95

Writing for Children & Teenagers, by Lee Wyndham (paper) $9.95

Writing for Regional Publications, by Brian Vachon $11.95

Writing for the Soaps, by Jean Rouverol $14.95

Writing to Inspire, by Gentz, Roddy, et al $14.95

The Writing Business

Complete Guide to Self-Publishing, by Tom & Marilyn Ross $19.95

Complete Handbook for Freelance Writers, by Kay Cassill $14.95

Editing for Print, by Geoffrey Rogers $14.95

Freelance Jobs for Writers, edited by Kirk Polking (paper) $7.95

How to Be a Successful Housewife/Writer, by Elaine Fantle Shimberg $10.95

How to Get Your Book Published, by Herbert W. Bell $15.95

How to Understand and Negotiate a Book Contract or Magazine Agreement, by Richard Balkin $11.95

How You Can Make $20,000 a Year Writing, by Nancy Hanson (paper) $6.95

Literary Agents: How to Get & Work with the Right One for You, by Michael Larsen $9.95

The Writer's Survival Guide: How to Cope with Rejection, Success and 99 Other Hang-Ups of the Writing Life, by Jean and Veryl Rosenbaum $12.95

To order directly from the publisher, include $2.00 postage and handling for 1 book and 50¢ for each additional book. Allow 30 days for delivery.

Writer's Digest Books, Department B
9933 Alliance Road, Cincinnati OH 45242
Prices subject to change without notice.